Calm Surrender

By Kent Nerburn

A Haunting Reverence

Letters to My Son

Make Me an Instrument of Your Peace

Neither Wolf nor Dog

Simple Truths

Small Graces

Road Angels

Edited by Kent Nerburn

Native American Wisdom

The Soul of an Indian

The Wisdom of the Great Chiefs

The Wisdom of the Native Americans

Calm Surrender

Walking the Path of Forgiveness

KENT NERBURN

NEW WORLD LIBRARY
NOVATO, CALIFORNIA

New World Library
14 Pamaron Way
Novato, California 94949

Copyright © 2000 by Kent Nerburn
Cover design: Mary Beth Salmon
Cover photograph: Photonica

Library of Congress Cataloging-in-Publication Data

Nerburn, Kent, 1946–

Calm Surrender : walking the path of forgiveness / Kent Nerburn.

p. cm.

ISBN 1-57731-218-X

1. Forgiveness—Religious aspects—Christianity. 1. Title.

BV4647.F55 N47 2000

234'.5—dc21   99-042245

First paperback printing, April 2002
ISBN 1-57731-218-X

Printed in Canada on acid-free, partially recycled paper
Distributed to the trade by Publishers Group West

10 9 8 7 6 5 4 3 2 1

In memory of my grandfather,

Kent Charles Crofoot,

who loved stray dogs

Contents

Introduction: The Little Spotted Dog   ix

Chapter 1:   More Than I Had Hoped,   23
                   Less Than I Had Dreamed

Chapter 2:   Welcome Home   39

Chapter 3:   Calm Surrender   53

Chapter 4:   The Headache   65

Chapter 5:   The Message Tree   79

Chapter 6:   Candles on the Grave   95

Chapter 7:   Poisoned Waters   107

Chapter 8:   An Embrace of the Heart   125

Epilogue: Max & Shrimp   135

Then Peter came up and said to Jesus, "Lord, how often shall my brother sin against me and I forgive him? As many as seven times?" Jesus said to him, "I do not say to you seven times, but seventy times seven."

Matthew 18:21–22

The Passover of the Jews was at hand, and Jesus went up to Jerusalem. In the temple he found those who were selling oxen and sheep and pigeons, and the money-changers at their business. And making a whip out of cords, he drove them all, with their sheep and oxen, out of the temple; and he poured out the coins of the money-changers and overturned their tables.

John 2:13–15

Introduction

The Little Spotted Dog

❧

Not long ago, I received a letter from my old friend John, with whom I had not corresponded in some time. He is several years younger than I, and perhaps for that reason has always looked to me for advice when his life has taken a confusing turn. On this occasion, he had decided to write me because of a disquieting event that had occurred several days before.

He, like me, is a father. And he, like me, struggles to raise his children to serve the common good, rather than simply promote their own self interests and personal accomplishments. It is a difficult challenge, but one in which we both believe.

The event that had prompted him to write was not one of great significance in the world, but it had touched him deeply. He and his young daughter had been walking down an alley near their home on the way to the store, when they had come upon a little spotted dog, badly undernourished, chained to a fence on a leash no more than two feet long. The dirt under the dog's feet was worn into a bowl; the dog itself was wide-eyed, frantic, and hysterical. Nearby, a water and food dish were tipped over. They were covered with dust, and obviously had not been filled for several days.

John looked up at the house. It was ill-kept, with a broken screen door. Music was blaring from inside, and there were motorcycles parked among piles of beer cans and trash on the expanse of dirt and weeds that had once been a lawn.

Cautiously, he and his daughter approached the dog. It was still friendly, even desperately so. They looked in the dog's eyes; the dog looked back at them with terror and yearning. They petted the dog and hugged it. The dog pulled at its leash and wagged its tail frantically.

"Suddenly, we both began crying," he wrote. "That little dog was pushing against us like we were his only hope in the world. We just sat there hugging it and crying while the little dog shivered in our arms."

John thought of approaching the house and confronting the owners, but he was afraid. He thought of stealing the dog, but was concerned that if he got caught the dog's owners might harm him or his child. Besides, he thought, even if he were successful, these people would just get another dog and abuse it the same way.

His daughter looked at him, wide-eyed and hopeful. "What should we do, Dad?" she asked him.

"I don't know," he mumbled. "I'll think of something."

But he couldn't. Unable to come up with any reasonable response, he turned away and continued walking down the alley. Behind them, the little spotted dog barked and yipped and pulled at its chain, as if begging them to come back and save it.

"My cheeks burned with shame," he wrote. "I tried to hide my tears from my girl, but it was like some floodgate had been opened. It wasn't just the dog. I could call the animal control people, and they'd probably take care of it. But what about all the other little dogs? What about all the old people trapped in their houses like dogs chained to fences because they're afraid to go out on the street? What about all the misery and cruelty we see in the world around us every day? That little pup broke my heart, but it was just the last straw, a pitiful symbol of everything heartless and cruel in this world."

I understood too well what he was talking about. The harshness and cruelty of the world weigh on my heart, too. The mother swatting at her wide-eyed and hopeful child as he makes an innocent request in the supermarket, the incomprehensible murders and brutalities that scream at us from the headlines every day, even the simple incivilities we bear in our daily dealings with others often leave me trapped somewhere between frustration and rage.

But my friend wasn't done. His next few lines brought me up short. "I get sick of all the weak-kneed sermonizing I hear about forgiveness," he wrote. "All this talk about turning the other cheek and how we need to ignore the negative and try to find the positive in everything, about how the world is perfect in its abundance if we only know how to look at things. Just once I'd like one of those 'perfect world' people to walk down that alley with me and look into that little dog's terrified eyes. I'd like them to tell me about the positive in that situation. I'd like them to show me what good I do by turning the other cheek on that little spotted dog."

The letter went on to more trivial issues, but I wasn't really paying attention. My friend had struck a nerve, and his questions haunted me.

How do we deal with cruelty and evil in this world when we are taught to turn the other cheek and to forgive not seven times, but seventy times seven? How do we acknowledge the darkness of life without becoming ensnared in it? What is the true shape of honorable forgiveness?

I had no easy answers. But I wanted to write back. Finally, as evening came, I sat down to write a response.

❧

John —

It was good to hear from you. Your letters always brighten my day. But this one also burdened me, because it asked me to confront an issue that haunts me every day as I try to raise a child to a worthy manhood in this strange and confusing time. What is the shape of an honorable forgiveness, and how do we pass it along to those entrusted to our care?

Everywhere we look the world seems awash in unspeakable cruelties. Innocent people are murdered for no reason at all. The elderly are prisoners in their own homes, afraid to go out on the streets. Children starve in far-off lands, while countries that claim to be civilized debate the merits of sending them food. Governments blow off people's limbs with land mines in the name of peace and freedom, then send them crutches and call it compassion. The list is endless, and, with every revelation, the caring heart breaks a little more.

Are we really supposed to turn the other cheek and walk away from these cruelties in the name of forgiveness? Are we really supposed to love the perpetrators of these acts?

The great-hearted among us — the Nelson Mandelas, Martin Luther Kings, Gandhis — would argue that we must. Shower the offenders with love, they say. Bathe them in the healing light of unqualified forgiveness, for against such a light a darkness cannot stand.

And, for them, it works. The spiritual force and clarity of their vision makes them glow with an inner peace that gives their acts of forgiveness an active, transformative power.

But we are not Nelson Mandela, Martin Luther King, or Gandhi. We are ordinary people, just trying to get by in our lives. When we try to practice forgiveness as an act of absolution, it doesn't seem to spread out and enlighten those around us. On the contrary, it often seems to be nothing more than tacit acquiescence to the world's cruelty and injustice. The cruel and brutish people who throw beer cans in their yards just ignore us or laugh at us, and the little spotted dog remains hungry and frightened and chained to a fence.

What are we to do? We both know that most people we meet are kind and caring, and trying to do good in the world. But the cruelty and violence all around us seems to have a dark and active presence that feeds upon itself. It laughs at the efforts of kind and caring people to create a world of compassionate humanity.

Should the rape victim be expected to forgive the rapist? Is the mother of a murdered child supposed to forgive the murderer? What about the man who can't buy shoes for his children because his company has sent his job overseas, while the executives who made the decision take home six-figure bonuses? Should these people turn the other cheek and walk away? Or should they demand justice and fight against the wrong with the heart of a warrior?

I often think of a neighbor of mine — a good, church-going woman — whose husband died of a hereditary disease in the prime of life. One month he was fine; the next he was moving slowly, struggling for breath; the next, he was in the hospital so weak that he couldn't roll over without assistance. His disease affected only his lungs — the rest of him was the picture of health. He needed only a lung transplant to return to being the involved community member, good father, loving husband, and dear friend that he had always been.

But he was unable to get the transplant, and, eventually, despite the efforts of many people on his behalf, he died. On the surface, it would seem that he merely fell victim to a cruel twist of circumstance. More people needed lungs than there were donors, and his number did not come up in time.

But it wasn't that simple. In the course of the man's desperate efforts to receive a lung, he decided to use his personal savings to publicize his plight. "If it helps me get a lung," he reasoned, "that would be wonderful. But even if it doesn't, by putting a human face on the need for donor organs, perhaps I can raise public awareness. And if I can help just one more person receive the gift of life, it will be money well spent."

But the networks in charge of organ distribution didn't see it that way. The more he tried to publicize his plight, the greater the subtle pressure, he encountered to stop. When friends and concerned people tried to dig into the reasons behind this pressure some profoundly seamy truths about the system of organ distribution began to be uncovered. What had on the surface seemed to be simply a shortage of donor organs soon revealed itself as a snake pit of competing health care systems, hospital turf wars, regional organ distribution fiefdoms, and a host of behind-the-scenes economic and political machinations.

In the end, though it could never be proved, or even confidently asserted, it was not entirely clear that the man's efforts on his own behalf were not in some way responsible for him never receiving the donor organ.

After the funeral, his grieving wife chose the route

of pure, unqualified forgiveness. From the goodness of her heart, she focused on how her husband's death had brought their family closer, and on the good his own organs would do for others. She celebrated the goodness in his life, celebrated the positive aspects of his death, and set about working to raise awareness of the organ donor program in our community.

To all initial appearances, she seemed to have taken the highest road possible by finding the good in a personal tragedy. But by taking the path of forgiveness as tacit acceptance of what had occurred, had she not in some way been complicit in the continuation of a system that might really need to be confronted? Did her celebration of the goodness that came from her husband's death best serve the spirit of forgiveness? Or would forgiveness have been better served if she had used her own heart-wrenching odyssey to reveal, blow by blow, the suspect operations of a system that holds the power of life and death in its hands, and wields it without scrutiny?

There is no easy answer. By becoming an advocate for organ donation, this good woman is now increasing the awareness of people around the country of the need to make the organs of their loved ones available on their death. But she is also cementing another block in an edifice that often operates with suspect procedures and practices behind a wall of secrecy.

I cannot judge my neighbor's actions. Grief takes its own course, and we all must do what is necessary to free ourselves from its pain. She did what her heart commanded, and it is helping her heal. That, for her, is the first and deepest task.

But the next person, denied an organ for reasons never revealed or satisfactorily explained, may not be so sanguine about her choice. That person may say that she has become a willing footsoldier in a rogue general's army, and that her acquiescence has made their mission harder.

This is the dilemma that faces us all when we decide to walk the difficult path of forgiveness. Are we complicit in wrongdoing if we do not challenge those who wrong us? Or are we contributing to the darkness in the world if we get caught up in the web of heartlessness and cruelty that gave birth to the injustice?

I don't know. And yet I must know. Somehow, I, you, each of us, must find a way to respond to the cruelty and injustice in the world in a way that doesn't empower those who harm others. At the same time, we must avoid becoming ensnared by their anger and heartlessness.

One of the great human wagers is whether we best achieve this by shining a light of pure absolution into the darkness, trusting that the light will draw others toward it, or whether we stand against the darkness with equal force, and then try to flood the world with light once the darkness is held at bay.

In either case, though, one thing is certain: Forgiveness cannot be a disengaged, pastel emotion. It is demanded in the bloodiest of human circumstances, and it must stand against the strongest winds of human rage and hate. To be a real virtue, engaged with the world around us, it must be muscular, alive, and able to withstand the outrages and inequities of inhuman and inhumane acts. It must be able to face the dark side of the human condition.

How we shape such forgiveness is one of the most crucial questions in our lives. And, it is not easy. Sometimes we get so frustrated that we don't think we can take it any more.

But we can and we must; it is our human responsibility. Even though we know that forgiveness, misused, or misunderstood, can become a tacit partner in the wrongs around us, we also know that, properly applied, it is the glue that holds the human family together. It is the way to bridge the loneliness that too often surrounds us. We must find a way to build that bridge, even if our hands are clumsy and the materials at our command are flawed.

And so, my friend, I don't have an easy answer. All I can do is counsel you to struggle forward, and take solace in the example of Jesus. In one breath, he counseled us to turn the other cheek and forgive our enemies "seventy times seven." In the next, he was excoriating the money changers and chasing them from the temple.

If even he, so close to God, struggled so greatly with the issue of forgiveness, who are we to think that we shouldn't have to do the same?

Write back soon.

Your friend,
Kent

❧

I didn't hear from John for about two weeks. But one day I arrived home to find a letter in my mailbox. It had no return address, but I recognized the familiar handwriting. I opened it hurriedly, excited to read what he had to say.

Inside was a single folded sheet of paper on which was written one short paragraph.

"Gods and saints are fine. We all need to gaze up at the stars. But what about those of us slogging through the muck of everyday life? What do we tell our children about forgiveness? How do we justify little spotted dogs chained to a fence? You write books. You have a son. Someone needs to speak to this. Why not you? Why not now?"

That was it. No more.

And so this book was born. It is not a how-to book of spiritual advancement, or a book of easy answers to hard questions. It is the thoughts and reflections of an ordinary man as he walks through the ordinary landscape of everyday life in search of a path of forgiveness. It is a search for the elusive angels of compassion and understanding while wrestling with the devils of cruelty, anger, and injustice. I hope all of you who travel with me will find it a journey worth taking.

*If we cannot see the good in ourselves,
we will not see the good in others.*

Chapter 1

More Than I Had Hoped,
Less Than I Had Dreamed

❧

He who has faults is forgiven.
Tao Te Ching

That which I am, I would not; that which I would, I do not.
St. Paul, Romans 7:13.

*F*orgiving ourselves is the wellspring of all true forgiveness. It is the deep work of the heart that allows us
to grow toward the light instead of struggling constantly
with the darkness. Yet, it is also one of the most difficult tasks we face, because we very often are unaware
of the thorns and brambles that hold our heart captive.

But what does this really mean? Let me tell you a
story.

When I was a child, my father served as the direc-
tor of disaster services for the local chapter of the
American Red Cross. His job was to provide food and
clothing to those whose lives had been ravaged by
fires, tornadoes, floods, and those events insurance
companies darkly call "acts of God."

It was a job with no politics and no agenda. The

same radio calls that alerted the police and fire departments alerted my father. The same sense of immediacy was at the heart of his mission. He arrived at the scenes of death and destruction almost simultaneously with those whose job it was to quell the flames, stanch the flow of blood, fight back the waters, pick up the pieces.

And from an early time in my life, I went with him. Late at night, from deep in my sleep, I would hear the distant sound of a ringing telephone, and soon I would see the light in the hallway come on. My father would open my door a crack and say, "There's a four alarm on the northside." He never asked me if I wanted to come along, but we both knew what he meant.

Often I was too tired, or simply disinterested. But usually I forced myself to get out of bed and tag along. I wanted him to be proud of me, and I wanted to be with him, though often we would barely speak as we made our way through the empty, late-night city streets. My eyes would be heavy, and I would be tempted to sleep. But the sense of anticipation, the curiosity about what we would confront, kept me awake. Usually, my father would give me small tasks, like writing down the time of the phone call or making sure his clipboard contained the correct forms and disbursing orders. I would struggle with the bumps and bounces of the speeding car as I tried to mimic the almost uncanny neatness of his script. And when we arrived, I would walk around carrying his clipboard or some other bit of equipment, trying to seem important and involved.

Often we would arrive to find a smoldering pile of rubble. The family would already have gone to stay with relatives, and all that was left was the acrid smell of wet ash and smoke, and the weary banter of exhausted firemen as they wound up hoses and departed for the firehouse to grab a few hours sleep before the next alarm.

But other times we would walk into a cataclysm of human suffering. A plane crash where a small body was carried past on a stretcher with one charred and almost unrecognizable foot sticking out from under the sheet; a fire in a tenement where an old woman sat next to me sobbing and begging the beleaguered firemen to go back into the burning building to save her seventeen-year-old cat, her only friend and companion in the world — these are the memories that filled my nights.

It is hard to explain the disorientation that took place in my heart as I followed my father's footsteps. I would go to bed in a warm and protected house, then, in the middle of the night, be yanked from my sleep and transported to some scene of unspeakable tragedy, then wake the next morning back in the comfortable bed I had snuggled into the night before.

Was it all a dream? Did it really happen? My mind told me it did — the images of emergency lights and sirens and flames rising a hundred feet into the sky were burned like scars into my memory. But the smell of breakfast cooking downstairs and the bustlings of two little sisters getting ready for school made it all seem distant, inconceivable. It was almost too much for my young spirit to fathom.

Year after year this strange emotional bifurcation was a central part of my life. By day, I was a young boy, worried about my complexion, whether I would make the basketball team, or if some girl liked me. By night I was intimate witness to all manner of human tragedy and suffering.

On first consideration, this breadth of experience would seem to have been beneficial to my development. It increased my sense of compassion and social responsibility, and made me aware of the small and protected world in which most of us live our lives.

But underneath, deep in my spirit, something else was going on. Slowly, inexorably, I was developing a kind of self-loathing that was running to the very core of my being. How could I possibly be concerned with my own happiness when all around me people were dying, losing loved ones, and having their lives shattered by the most horrifying and disastrous events?

How could I possibly think it was important

whether my hair looked good when the night before I had seen the bloated body of a boy my age pulled from a lake skewered on the end of a grappling hook?

The legitimacy of my entire notion of self was being called into question. Even the most humble and natural aspirations I had for myself: love, family, any dream of achievement, became to me symptoms of self-absorption and my own spiritual deficiency.

Without knowing it, I became a monk in my heart. I would go out every evening after supper and walk for hours with only my old dog for companionship. Fields, darkened golf courses, marshes, became my monastery. I would wander alone through the night, wrestling with the demons of adolescence and trying to fight off my desperate yearnings for love and comfort.

Gradually, on those evening walks, I evolved an entire philosophy of spiritual asceticism on which to base my life. I came to believe that the only way to truly enter another's feelings was to have no attachments or desires of my own. In that way I could become transparent to the circumstances of others. I could enter their emotional reality without the intrusion of my own desires and good fortune.

It made sense. If I had no emotional home where I could feel warm and protected, I wouldn't be able to retreat there, in my own spirit, when I confronted the sadness and tragedy of another person with no home. If

I had no self to protect, I could empathize completely with another's pain and suffering.

I was a shaman of the spirit, emptying myself so that I could take the pain and suffering of another into me, so that they might not be alone in their moment of tragedy.

Unfortunately, unlike the real shaman, I had no way to spit out the poison of that tragedy. It lodged inside of me and filled me with shame for every happiness or desire I experienced.

It wasn't until years later that the simplest realization came to me. I was sitting alone in a cafe watching a couple at another table. They were in the full blush of fresh love, leaning close to each other, touching each other's hair, looking longingly into each other's eyes. My heart ached for what they had, but I steeled myself against my own desires, and comforted myself with the thought that my heart was better able to feel the emotions of others because I was free of the limited and self-referential warmth of a private and personal love.

As I got up to leave, and cast one final glance at the couple, I was struck by something that I should have realized years before. Their emotional reality was every bit as real as that of those suffering in the world, yet I was not trying to enter their reality; instead, I was demeaning it and defending against it.

In that instant I had this overwhelming realization

that my self-abnegation and denial did not allow me to embrace and enter into the happiness and joys of others, but only into their loneliness and suffering. Unconsciously, and very likely as a response to the traumatic events that had unfolded before me as a child, I had convinced myself that happiness was transience and illusion, an unworthy aspiration for anyone seeking meaningful spiritual growth. Sadness and tragedy were, for me, the baseline human reality — the undeniable truth that lay beneath each moment of brightness and light. The great ascetic edifice I was building was really a philosophical house of cards that kept me from accepting and embracing any of my own desire for warmth and happiness.

I'm sure I could have taken this hard-won vehicle of self-denial and fine-tuned it into a lifelong pursuit of an ascetic ideal. But, at heart, I didn't want that for myself. I wanted home, I wanted family, I wanted love. I wanted all the messy clutter of human reality. The calm clarity of emotional disengagement was not the spiritual path I truly wanted to travel.

I have now spent the better part of my adult life working through this issue, and I am gradually allowing myself to seek happiness and satisfaction in my own life. I am still too quick to see the darkness, too willing to see the good in the world as illusion and to look upon moments of peace and tranquility as small islands of respite in a sea of tragedy. But I now know this about myself, and I can guard against it.

I now look back in wonder at all the pain I caused myself and others as I constructed this artful self-justification around my worldview and actions. I was convinced it was not only legitimate, but noble. But behind it lay a heart that could not forgive itself.

Most of us have some corner where we cannot forgive ourselves. Sometimes it is obvious: the mother who leaves her child unattended for a moment and the child wanders into the street and a terrible death, the son who refuses to speak to his parents for years and realizes his errors only after they are gone.

But sometimes it is more subtle, and well buttressed with explanations and rationalizations: The abortion was necessary because we had neither the financial nor the emotional resources to bring another child into the world. The divorce was the only way to free two hearts from a destructive downward spiral. The harsh words we said to our children were for their own good. The time we spent at our job rather than with our family was necessary to provide them with the quality of life they deserved.

Perhaps our decisions were right, or necessary, or inevitable. Perhaps they were capricious and unwarranted. But we made them, and they are now and forever part of our lives. Still, our hearts ache for the choices made or denied, and we bury that ache beneath a blanket of guilt or high-minded justifications.

We need to find the hidden corners of our lives where we have not forgiven ourselves — for who we are, for who we are not. And it is not always easy. Sometimes we have to dig through tragic emotional wreckage. Sometimes we have to rip open scars we think have long been healed. Sometimes we have to tear down beautifully crafted psychological edifices. But to live with a pure heart and open spirit, we must have the courage to face these challenges.

Human beings are strange and miraculous creations. From our first moment on earth we are hurtling toward uniqueness and individuation. We revel in that uniqueness, find our identity in that individuation. But this sense of our own uniqueness and singularity comes at a price. For, with every door of understanding that is opened by the circumstances or choices of our lives, a wealth of others are closed. The child surrounded by joy does not learn the same world as the child surrounded with sadness. The child filled with fear does not discover the same world as the child filled with curiosity. I didn't know the same world as a child whose father went out every day to officiate at weddings, or the same world as the child with no father present at all. Every nuance of character and circumstance shuts out possibility even as it reveals the world in growing clarity and fullness. We become who we are at the expense of who we are not.

Emotionally healthy people accept this individuation with a sense of humility. They know that we are children of chance, and that we must develop our lives and give thanks for the miracle of life as it has been handed to us. They celebrate their uniqueness — with all its possibilities and limitations — build upon it, and use it as a way to contribute to the rich tapestry of humanity.

Emotionally unhealthy people, on the other hand, do not so readily give thanks for the shape life takes. They turn against themselves, refusing to embrace who they are, and go through life with the sense that their world is not enough. They are not rich enough, they are not smart enough, they are not pretty enough; they haven't gotten the right chances, the breaks have all gone someone else's way. Quick to see any deficiency in their own situation, they are slow to celebrate the gifts life has given them. The miracle of their uniqueness becomes instead the prison of their limitations. They define themselves by what they are not.

Most of us, however, lie somewhere in between. We're reasonably happy with our lives, but look with longing at the road not taken. We retain a lifelong ambivalence about who we are, and never fully grasp the potential that our unique life experiences offer us. We see the smallness of our lives, not the greatness of our gifts, and feel deficient in relation to those we hold as models of success and accomplishment.

We must learn to resist this. Until we can embrace our lives wholeheartedly, aware of our limitations and committed to making the most of our unique circumstances and gifts, we have not fully accepted ourselves for the people we are, or fully forgiven ourselves for the people we are not.

I will never be Nelson Mandela, or Gandhi, or even the gentle, soft-spoken man down the street. I will never be as hardworking as my father. I will never be a mountain climber or a buddha or someone who bikes across the United States. I will never be a saint.

But I will always be a good listener, a faithful friend, a person whose word can be trusted. I will always stand by the weak and protect the innocent. But I will also be a person filled with righteous indignation at the injustices in the universe, a person prone to deep solitudes and possessed of a dark cast of spirit and perhaps overly aware that tragedy can strike in the middle of the night.

In short, I will be a person like everybody else — a unique and fallible human being, possessed of conflicting and sometimes contradictory characteristics, whose life is full of moments of brightness and moments of dark impenetrable shadow; a person at once more than I had hoped but less than I had dreamed.

I must learn to accept this person and to embrace him. I must learn to look at the unique constellation of skills and attributes I have, the strange character twists and quirks I've developed, the quality of my own passions and the subtlety of my own deceptions. I must learn to acknowledge my fears, respect my own dreams, and measure them only against the simple standard of how they help make this a better world for the people around me and the generations that come after me.

If I am able to do this, I will not try to be what I am not, but I will try to make the most of what I am. And, in doing this, I will forgive myself for all the possibilities that didn't take flower in me, and will honor them whenever I see them present in others.

This is the first and most necessary step upon the path of forgiveness. If I am not accepting of myself, all that is good in others will either be a mirror of my own deficiencies, or a cause of envy, or a way of life against which I must protect myself with cynicism or contempt.

Life cannot be lived this way. It is too short, too precious, too important. There are children out there who need my help; there is a family that relies on me for love. There are people I meet on the street and in chance encounters whose lives can be either better or worse for the moment's contact we share.

I must measure myself in these moments, not in some abstract valuation of my own spiritual accomplishments or against the accomplishments of others. I am who I am, and I must honor the vision of life I have been given. If that vision shuts out other people, I must work to change it. If it allows me to give and to open myself to others, I must foster it.

We are, to the best of our knowledge, given only one go-round on this earth. We are thrown together with a group of strangers who share our passage through time, and, together, we leave as a generation and become, both literally and figuratively, the soil on which future generations walk.

It is our responsibility, both singly and together, to prepare this earth for those who follow. The moments we confront in our lives will never be confronted by anyone else. The encounters we have are unique in this universe. All that we can do is meet the moments we have been granted with a humble and caring heart, and share the gifts we have been given with those whose lives brush against ours.

In this way — in this active claiming of our own fallible self, and shaping it for a life of service — we open our hearts to the possibility of forgiveness. Rather than railing against our deficiencies, or constructing justifications for them, we see them as part of our unique life and circumstances, and look for the moment when the unique person we are is needed, and offer ourselves in service, humbly, and like a prayer.

It is no crime to be less than our dreams, or to stumble and fall on life's path. The crime is in refusing to get up and move toward the light, or in being unwilling to embrace those around us who have fallen in their own way.

We will never be as good or worthy as we wish to be. We will be human — too human — and we will fall short of our hopes for ourselves over and over again. If we can forgive ourselves for our failures — not seven times, but seventy times seven — we can forgive others for their failures. We know that we are all humans, struggling by the lights we have toward our vision of good.

As I sit here now, I think of the life that might have been, and the man I longed to be. I see the hollow reed of pure spiritual consciousness, the instrument of God's peace, that I dreamed of being when I was a child. And I know that it was good.

But then I think of my family, with each of us struggling to find form, struggling to dream, struggling to make sense of the world around us, but always finding in our common love a solid rock on which to build our lives, and it, too, is good. That I have been given such a gift is humbling beyond words. A life of solitary spiritual rigor would have been different, but it would have been no more worthy.

I could not have dreamed this life, could not have invented it from the whole cloth of my imagination. It is a miracle in its uniqueness, a treasure of unexpected grace. Though I am not what I thought I should be, I am more than I might ever have hoped. As I survey the landscape of my life, I am overcome with a sense of wonder.

Somewhere, another man, much like me, may be living a life of pure spiritual consciousness, unencumbered with fragmentary personal emotions, able to enter the lives and hearts of those he meets because his own heart is empty of concern with self. But I am not that man. I walk the streets, full of loves and fears and angers and dreams, tethered to family and worldly cares. Yet I know, in my heart, that whenever there is a call in the night, I will rise from my sleep and offer such nourishment and consolation as I am able. It is the least I can do as thanks for the miraculous gift of life that has been given to me.

Apology can take many forms;
true forgiveness accepts them all.

Chapter 2

Welcome Home

❧

The greatest carver does the least cutting.
Tao Te Ching

As a child, I was raised to believe that apology meant publicly "owning up" to my mistakes. Caught stealing, caught lying, caught digging up a neighbor's yard or talking back to an adult, I was marched down to the person I had wronged and made to offer a formal verbal apology. I would stand, with eyes downcast, mumbling something about how sorry I was and how I would never do it again. The bright lights of social disapproval were aimed on me and left there until I withered. Then punishment or compensation was determined, a stern forgiveness was offered, and I was sent off, full of chagrin and humiliation, charged to "sin no more."

Without any conscious awareness of what was happening, this became the model of the apology for me — the one I expected from others, and the one I was expected to give. Anything less, I felt, left an incomplete seal on the acts of forgiving and being forgiven. Apology and contrition came to be inextricably involved with public declaration, even humiliation. Even if it meant standing before only one person — the one who had been wronged — an overt acknowledgment of the wrong was necessary.

But as I have gotten older I've come to distrust this approach, because it is built on a spiritual imbalance between the strength of the forgiver and the weakness of the one seeking forgiveness. Often it does more to emphasize sickness than to heal. A better way, it seems to me, is to offer forgiveness with a gentle, almost invisible touch.

This came home to me the other day when I went to visit my friend Bob, whom I hadn't seen for several months.

Bob lives alone with his old dog, L.B. He is a simple man in love with machines. His garage is filled with all manner of tools and electrical testing equipment. His greatest pleasure in life is to be given a mechanical problem that no one else has been able to solve, and to pore over every minute aspect of the offending machinery or circuitry until he has isolated the problem, then to deftly and efficiently set the machine right. There is nothing that, given enough time, he can't diagnose and repair. It doesn't matter if the offending mechanism is a fork lift or a computer — if there is a systematic underpinning to its operation, Bob can figure it out and fix it. And there is nothing in life he would rather do than make such repairs for people he cares about or people in need.

As a result of his skill and good-heartedness, his garage has become a haven for people besieged by the machines in their lives. On any given day you might find a local contractor who is having problems with the hydraulics of some earth moving equipment, or a college student who needs help getting his marginal vehicle back on the road, or a single mother who can't afford to take her car to a repair shop. But it doesn't matter who the person is, or their status in life; once inside Bob's garage they are his friends and their problem is his problem.

I used to visit Bob regularly. His home was on my route back from town, and my son loved to throw tennis balls for L.B. Because I wrote books and because I had more education than most of the people he knew, Bob viewed me with a certain amount of respect. It was a feather in his cap when I would stop by while some of his other friends were there. He would mention my books, discuss passages I had written, and generally take pride in his friendship with someone who he felt represented a higher level of intellectual achievement than he had attained.

The attention was a bit embarrassing, but I always

felt that if it made Bob happy, I was more than willing to oblige, especially for a man who gave so much of himself so willingly to others.

One of Bob's proudest possessions in life was an old BMW motorcycle. He liked to brag that he had put more than 100,000 miles on it and it still ran like new. Every Saturday night he would get on his bike and ride for miles through the pine-covered country near our home, stopping at local bars and restaurants and roadhouses.

Because he was on a motorcycle, and always willing to strike up a conversation with anyone, he soon found himself making friends with other motorcycle riders he met along the way. If they were having problems with one of their bikes, he would take out his bag of tools and fix it on the spot. If the problem was more serious, he would invite them to come by his home where he would do what he could to put the bike back in good repair.

Never one to charge much money, Bob drew people who didn't have much of it. He would take minimal payment if they had it, and would accept trades if they did not. Many of the people didn't have much cash. But many of them did have other things to offer. Soon Bob found himself being offered cocaine and other drugs in lieu of cash payments.

How much he accepted, or how willingly, I don't

know. But the word got out that Bob was a good mechanic who could fix things on the fly, that he was willing to horsetrade, and that he was always good for a meal or a beer or a place to stay. Gradually, like a subtle change in the weather, the people who hung out at his garage started to have a different feel.

When I would go by Bob's garage to visit, I began to find myself profoundly uncomfortable. The people hanging out there had a fundamental hiddenness about them. They offered little of themselves, always seemed on guard, and always appeared to be wanting something while offering nothing. They would stop their conversations when I entered, and would leave as quickly as they could. Clearly, they wanted no witnesses to whatever it was they had in common with Bob.

This was a far cry from the wood stove folksiness and *bonhomie* that had previously characterized his garage. And when our visits started being interrupted by short phone calls that were carried on in muffled tones and coded language, and were quickly followed by visits from people who would arrive and disappear in five minutes' time, it was clear that something bad was on the horizon.

Perhaps I should have done something. I did broach the issue of how things were starting to have the whiff of trouble about them. But Bob assured me that these were just people who were a little down on their luck and needed his help. He was just doing what he always did — helping the unfortunate — and he chided me for having so little faith in him as a judge of people and character.

Still, the feeling of his world had changed, and I no longer felt comfortable being part of it. I gradually withdrew from our friendship, assuming that our lives had begun to take different paths.

Then, several months ago, I picked up the morning paper and saw the headline I should have known was coming: "Major Drug Ring Smashed." Underneath was Bob's name. He was the only local person involved. He had been arrested in a motel parking lot with various drug paraphernalia under the seat of his truck. It was unclear what had happened, but it was clearly an unsavory situation, and Bob was right in the middle of it.

I followed the story in the local crime reports, and even gave some thought to contacting the courts to see if I could stand up for Bob as a character witness. Perhaps I could add some context and explain that beneath the seamy headlines and the furtive, nighttime dealings, was a simple, good-hearted man who had allowed himself to get swept up into a dangerous and illegal situation.

But I chose not to get involved. Each time I came close to acting, I would think of my young son, on the cusp of his teenage years, and think that Bob's mistake, so stupid and fundamentally harmless when kept in the confines of his own life, was potentially lethal when it spilled over into the lives of children like my boy.

I decided to let the legal system take its course. But Bob was still my friend, and no less the decent man I had known and often relied on so many times in the past. The least I could do was pay him a visit.

I found him in his garage. He was out on bail, awaiting trial. He looked older and more thoughtful than the last time I had seen him. Yes, he said, it was true. He had gotten himself in a bit of trouble. But he was quick to point out that these were not bad people — they, too, were ordinary men who had gotten in too deep. And though I was skeptical, as the story unfolded, I began to get a different picture than the one painted by the local paper.

He told of the long nights when he and his new friends would sit around his kitchen table sharing stories of the stupid choices they had made, and trying to figure out a way to get out of the lives they were living. He told me the stories of their backgrounds, of the lives they had thrown away.

A bad relationship, a lost job, the lure of easy money, and soon they had all found themselves on a downward slide toward exploiting other people, alienating their friends, and abusing the trust of those about whom they cared the most. Then he said the most poignant thing of all: "We all realized we were the kind of people we wouldn't want our children to be around."

There was really no response I could give. He had discovered the rock bottom truth about his actions and what he had become. But the fact was, he had become it, and there was now a price to be paid.

We went on with our conversation, mixing small talk about engines and fuel injectors with his occasional bursts of explanation and penitence. But it was clear that he was chagrined about the situation he had gotten himself into, and that he harbored a deep sense of personal shame about what he had done.

I listened sympathetically and added a few bland generalities about the lessons life teaches us and how we all learn from our mistakes, then gradually moved the conversation back to the superficialities of the day. Clearly, Bob was happy to leave the issue, and he animatedly showed me a new part he was fabricating for a forklift. Soon it was time for me to go.

But as I rose to leave, Bob's whole manner changed. He began thanking me effusively for coming. Over and over he kept telling me how much it meant that I had come to visit. I felt like I was talking to a prisoner who didn't want me to leave. And, in a way, I was. Bob had become a prisoner of his own sense of guilt, and in some deep and fundamental way, my visit had become in his mind an act of forgiveness.

He may not have known this consciously, but he

understood it in his heart. He knew he had done wrong, but he also knew that, in some way, he had to atone for his actions by publicly admitting his error and demonstrating his change of heart.

It might seem that I was far from the correct person to receive his admission. I had not been directly involved; my life had not been affected by his choices. And true forgiveness is found only in the embrace of those we have wronged. But, subconsciously, Bob understood something crucial about his actions. His greatest crime had been against himself. He had not sold drugs, he had simply used them and served as a clearinghouse for those who trafficked in them. The people he had wronged were, indeed, his old friends who had trusted him and had believed in his good heart and judgment. If there was a crime against anyone, other than himself, it was an abstract crime against the children of the world who are the prey of the people like those with whom he had surrounded himself.

By coming to me as a friend, he was asking forgiveness for betraying the faith his friends had placed in him. By coming to me as the father of the boy who had always loved visiting his house to play with his dog, he was asking forgiveness for the crimes in which his distant participation had possibly played a part.

It was a profoundly poignant gesture, and one that was hard for him to make. It did not involve groveling, or self-flagellation, or a great public declaration of contrition. It did not even involve saying, "I'm sorry." It simply involved laying himself bare in all his humiliation before someone who had the power to stand by him or to turn his back and walk away.

I chose to stand by him. Knowing Bob, it was easy to do. He may have been conning himself about the good-heartedness of his new friends, but he was not conning himself about the significance of his own participation. And he was not attempting to con me. He had learned a hard lesson, and telling his story to me, rather than hiding it from view, was his plaintive way of asking for forgiveness for his mistakes.

In another man, it might not have seemed like enough. But Bob was someone who made his living with actions, not words. His life was, at its best, a life of charitable gestures that were symbolic statements of love and concern. His willingness to drop what he was doing, even when it was a paying job, to help someone whose need was more immediate, was a more eloquent statement of care and compassion than anything he could possibly say.

Likewise, his quiet recounting of the wrong direction he had taken was as eloquent a plea for forgiveness as any great display of contrition he could make. If I had demanded a formal apology from him, I simply would have been shaming him, and Bob did not need to be shamed; he needed to be embraced and brought back into the good graces of those he felt he had betrayed.

Most of us are like Bob. When we make an error in judgment, we are acutely aware of our mistake. We do not need to be made to grovel. That simply reduces us to the status of supplicant, and, again, establishes an imbalance between us and the one from whom we are seeking forgiveness.

What we really need is to be ratified in the fullness of our being, and reminded that our mistake was just that — a mistake — and that even if it is central to our sense of self at that moment, it is only a momentary shadow across the fundamental goodness of our character.

This is the goal we must all have when others seek our forgiveness. We need to watch for the smaller, quieter acts that reveal their heart. The child who washes the dishes after being chastised for laziness or selfishness, the husband or wife who brings flowers after an argument is expressing contrition in a way that is every bit as profound as someone getting down on their knees and begging for forgiveness. If we have it in our hearts to accept these acts, we move toward healing much more surely than if we demand great and dramatic public apologies.

To be sure, some crimes are too great for such easy forgiveness, and for some people the offer of gentle forgiveness is nothing more than a license to go forth and continue acting in the same way. But, for most of us, the embrace of the person we have wronged is enough to fill us with gratitude and a commitment to do better in the future.

I chose to offer Bob this embrace. I shook his hand and told him I was glad things were starting to look up for him. We joked a bit, but there was no joking in his eyes. He was a man in a cage of his own creation, and my presence was a kind of absolution that only friendship could provide.

I left that day with new humility about the power of forgiveness I hold in my hands. How many people do I confront in the course of a day who are overcome with a sense of guilt or deficiency? Guilt for having done something wrong, guilt for being uninteresting, guilt for being old, guilt for not being pretty enough or rich enough or smart enough — there are a million sources of guilt — and even if those feelings are unjustified, they are no less real to those who have them.

When I meet such people, even in casual circumstances, by being present to them and caring about them, I am offering them forgiveness for the deficiencies they feel. I may not even realize I am offering forgiveness. And they may not even realize they are seeking forgiveness. But kindness and attentiveness is a kind of absolution that the suffering cannot give to themselves.

When we witness the good in someone, we offer them forgiveness for the hidden humiliations they feel inside. To show interest in someone who feels they have nothing to offer, to befriend the person who feels unlovable is more than an act of kindness. It is an act of forgiveness, because we are affirming their humanity, not shining light on their deficiencies.

One of the most poignant stories in the Bible is that of the prodigal son, who squandered his father's inheritance on prostitutes and high living, then, unable to survive any longer, went back to his father in shame. His father received him with joy, dressed him in the best clothes, and made a great feast for him. He did not berate him or lecture him or make his son's profligacy central in the forgiveness. He simply embraced his son and welcomed him home.

If we can remember this simple truth, and learn to act upon it, we will hold one of the greatest tools of forgiveness and healing in our hands. We will know that true forgiveness is not achieved by demanding that someone say they are sorry. True forgiveness is achieved when we embrace a person with our heart, and make them feel that in our presence they are welcomed home.

*By letting the small slights go, and
choosing to incline our hearts toward love,
we shape a life that reflects that love,
even if we do not live it every moment
of every day.*

Chapter 3

Calm Surrender

❜

$\mathcal{I}$ once had a student — a young Ojibwe boy — who always kept his heart hidden from view. He was not a bad kid, nor in any way a problem to anyone. He simply could not be reached when he decided to recede. He would stay home from school for reasons he wouldn't explain; he would disappear into his own interests and refuse to be involved with other activities until he saw fit to do so. He was always affable, but always unreachable. One day his mother made a comment that has stayed with me. "He is so private," she said. "Sometimes I have to look at the landscape all around him to figure out what is going on."

It was a wonderful observation, and full of insight. But, more than that, it offered me an image that has helped me understand another kind of challenge that faces the forgiving heart.

We all are born into a landscape — physical, emotional, economic, spiritual — not of our choosing. We build on that landscape, we explore, we change what we can. But we can never fully escape, nor can we fully reshape, the landscape into which we're born. It is our gift, and our burden.

What are we to do when the fundamental shape of that landscape offers us injustice or unfairness?

I receive a lesson in this kind of forgiveness every time I go to visit my mother. She lives alone in a high-rise apartment complex for the elderly. It is not the situation I would dream for her; in a better world she would live among children and families, in a home of her own with a garden and birds and animals that come to her window. But this world is what it is, and she is truly among the blessed of her generation: she doesn't live in fear and poverty, my father's pension allows her to live in relative comfort, she has caring children nearby, and though her body is failing her, her spirit has not been hardened by the indignities of age.

She was born eighty-two years ago. Her childhood is now reduced to stories, grown firmer and more important with each telling, like lights burning fiercely in a darkening room.

Her childhood seems to have taken place in a different age. Electricity and all its offshoots were novelties. Horse-drawn "sheeney" carts still came down the city streets calling for rags and bottles, and an ice man still brought great frozen blocks in chests so families could buy food that would stay fresh for more than a day.

Space was different then, too. People lived on blocks, walked to friends' houses, grew up and old with the same neighborhood friends. Parents spoke in foreign accents, or without English altogether, and each night men walked home from rough-hand jobs and put on white shirts before they sat down at the table to dinner.

Her father, my grandfather, was such a man — kind, gentle, a lover of dogs and music, and a drunk. He worked all day as a butcher, then came home to a house with no sons, bathed the blood from his hands, buttoned up his white shirt, and drank. His great dream was to one day travel the five hundred miles to the city of Chicago. But that dream never came to pass.

His two daughters orbited about him. He was the center, the father, the god. But he was also the little boy, lugubrious, who fell asleep on church steps when he drank too much, and had to be hauled from corner taverns before his paycheck disappeared into the hands of less scrupulous men, while his family — foodless, ashamed, and gossiped about by neighbors — waited at home.

It was my mother, the eldest, who had to go to the taverns and take his paycheck from him, so her mother could pay the bills and rent. And when she didn't get there soon enough, the family went without, and was evicted, and moved again, to a new place, where he would take a new job and start a new life.

Yet with each move nothing changed but the girls, who grew toward womanhood and dreams of freedom.

But for women it was not a time of freedom. Get married, prepare the dinner, keep the shirts ironed, and wait for the husband to get home. There was no other way. And my mother, so smart, so wounded, so full of her father's shame, succumbed.

There was that one shining moment when, in her early twenties, she got on a train and, against her parents' wishes, traveled to Washington, D.C. to take a job with the navy. Even now there is a light in her eyes when she talks about the days working at the Naval Observatory, the nights going out dancing with white-uniformed officers, the time she stood among the throngs and watched the pomp and grandeur of Roosevelt's second inauguration.

For that moment, she was at the center, anonymous and thrilled, not on the periphery, stared at and ashamed. There was no one to haul back from bars, no well-worn dress to wash every night so she would be clean, if ragged, when she went to school the following day. She was young, alive, and full of hope, and the world spread out before her.

But eventually, the times and her shame claimed her. A woman's place was in the home and near her family. It was children and kitchens and ironing and duty. A good woman was a good wife and mother. Without that, she was cast adrift.

And my mother did not want to be cast adrift. She had been adrift her entire life — the outsider, the outcast, the girl who thought her nose and feet were too big, the new girl in town, the daughter of the drunk. The girl waving from the train had to be left behind; in its place, the dutiful mother, the dutiful daughter, the dutiful wife, had to emerge.

So, when my father came courting, and her family thought so highly of him, she acquiesced and married. He was the other side of the excitement: He was the solidity, the security, and slowly he took the light of adventure from her eyes. It was all so understandable. He was no less wounded than she, and his need met hers. The eldest of seven children, he had been called back from his job at a summer camp at seventeen to find a family left parentless by the sudden, untimely death of his mother. His father — like hers, an alcoholic — had been gone for years; he walked out one day and never returned, leaving behind both physical and spiritual scars, and a sense of abandonment that none of the children would ever escape.

So, when that call came, and he rushed back in a

borrowed car, he was already the man, prepared to take the family and hold it tight. But he was also the little boy, abandoned by his father, now without his mother. He came back to a house looted and empty, his brothers and sisters taken to orphanages and foster homes.

Now he, too, was adrift. He wandered the streets, sleeping in church basements, walking miles to see his brothers and sisters — a little boy thrust into manhood, just as my mother, the eldest daughter, sent to drag home the singing drunken father and his paycheck, had been thrust too soon into womanhood.

So when the two of them met, it could hardly have been otherwise. Need met need, and two drifting ships found a common shore. Love? Yes, I am sure. But more than that, a family, secure, without beatings, without deaths, without the spore of alcohol around every corner. If my mother, in her heart, still dreamed of freedom, it didn't matter. Each bird must choose its cage, and, with her parents' promptings and my father's urgings, she chose hers.

Small wonder, then, that as a child I would sneak down and see her sitting at the table with distance in her eyes. One moment pulled toward security and respectability, the next toward freedom and dreams. There were no more tinkling glasses and men in pressed suits, only dirty dishes and baskets full of laundry.

If she did the washing, she did so without interest.

If she ironed, she did so without a sense of pride. There was no virtue for her in a flattened seam; her eyes were fixed on distant ports. Had she been born rich, and with confidence, she could have been Amelia Earhart, Beryl Markham, Anne Morrow Lindbergh. But she was born poor, an outsider, and ashamed of the home from which she had come. Though her dreams remained great, her life became small.

But she muddled through, smoking cigarettes at neighbors' kitchen tables and rushing home to put together suppers for a husband and a family that never knew or cared about the cage that life had built around her.

Other women, more content, more industrious, less filled with frustration at being indentured to an ironing board, cast her deficiencies in high relief, and once again the shame claimed her, and made her, in her own eyes, the flawed one, the watched one, the rejected, and the scorned.

So she gathered her family close around her and claimed it as her fiefdom. With guilt, orders, love, and intellect, she goaded and controlled and directed each of us toward honor and respect. There would be no shame in this family, no wounded hearts.

We each grew to adulthood, taking our separate paths, stained with the blood knowledge of being alone, different, isolated. We married, had children, watched her life reach an apogee, and decline. Our father, her husband, retired unrespected from a life of serving others, and without a moment's consideration of the dreams still alive in her, drew the boundaries of his life at the boundaries of his yard. Then, gradually, his physical and mental powers declined until his own mind became a mystery to him, and he wandered in its corridors like a stranger in an unknown room.

He became silent, distant, withdrawn. The endless service of his needs became her only job. Once again she was tethered to a man-boy, and like all other tasks that tied her to the domestic, she did it while holding back tears for the life that might have been.

But she did it, and she did it well. And when time claimed him, she was hurtled, frightened and confused, into the first true freedom her life had offered since her halcyon days in Washington. But this time there were no presidential inaugurations and military balls. There were knee replacements, and unsteady steps, and worries about failing eyesight, health, furnaces, and roofs. Her life became a daily struggle of the body, where before it had been a daily struggle of the spirit.

But during this time, something amazing happened. She embraced her life and forgave its limitations. The anger she felt at having been born out of time and thrust into a life that was too small for her dreams began to fade, and was replaced with a willing embrace of the momentary and immediate.

Yes, the flashes are still there. And the hurt of paths never pursued and vistas never explored surfaces at times, and drives her toward despair. But mostly, she has made her peace with her life and God. And she has done so without an obsessive focus on minutiae, instead staying present to the larger issues in the world while managing the daily bouts of immobility and pain.

It is a wondrous thing to see, and instructive to us all. Those things that earlier were entrapments — children, family, small responsibilities — are now pleasures, even joys. She has set her sights on closer horizons and has found in them a solace she never knew before.

Confucius once said that it is the wise person who can see near and far as the same and does not despise the small or value the great. Somehow, in the passage of her life, my mother has come to understand this wisdom, and has let go of those youthful dreams that left her so full of want and yearning. With the passing of time, her deep love of her father has erased her shame at his alcoholism. The memories of the good moments with her husband have washed away the anger and frustration at his stolid rootedness. Her children, the memories of her friends at kitchen tables, the trips she took, so small compared to her dream journeys, have become worthy destinations in her memory.

She has come to something close to gratitude in her understanding of life, and in this gratitude, she has forgiven, and she has been granted the peace of forgiveness. What a fruitful peace it is.

When that which has wronged us is too large or indifferent to reach out to us with a forgiving heart — the world, God, fate, whatever we choose to call it — the only path to forgiveness is through learning to see that world with different eyes. The world will not change; we must change. We must find a way to replace yearning for what life has withheld with gratitude for what we have been given.

I have long believed that the prayer we should carry constantly in our heart is, "Thank you, God, for the gift of life," because life is a gift given to us all, and is a mystery beyond all understanding. Once we have learned to look with equal joy upon the movements of a butterfly as we do upon travel to distant lands, we can forgive the world for those things it has withheld from us. After all, when we look back, aren't our mornings at a table with a dearly loved friend every bit as precious as our travels to distant destinations? It is only the sense of scale that differs.

And if we realize that our dreams are illusions of our own making, we can replace them with other, closer, more easily attainable dreams. For our satisfaction lies in the fulfillment of our dreams, no matter their size and scope.

This is the lesson that my mother seems to have learned.

The great Sioux thinker Ohiyesa once wrote, "Whenever, in the course of our day, we might come upon a scene that is strikingly beautiful or sublime — the black thundercloud with the rainbow's glowing arch above the mountain; a white waterfall in the heart of a green gorge; a vast prairie tinged with the blood-red of sunset — we pause for an instant in the attitude of worship."

My mother has learned to pause in an attitude of worship before the simple moments of her life, valuing the near as surely as the far. She has looked back over the landscape of her life — a landscape not of her making, and so much less than the landscape of her dreams — and she has seen that it is good.

She, who once lived as hostage to her dreams, now lives each day as an act of thanks for the miraculous gift of life.

Is there really more to forgiveness than this?

A seed of hope can become the flower of forgiveness.

Chapter 4

The Headache

˒

To know when to stop
To know when you can get no further by your own action
this is the right beginning.
— Chuang Tzu

𝒲e all know in our hearts that the litany of small, daily hurts — the friend who fails to call, the child who is unappreciative, the clerk who treats us brusquely, the spouse who fails to understand us — are the honest failings of ordinary people, and it is our task to rise above our immediate emotional reactions to respond with charity and love.

But even the most committed among us have moments when we feel no forgiveness in our hearts. Perhaps we are betrayed by a friend, abused by a family member, rejected by someone we trusted. Or maybe we have witnessed wanton cruelty, or been its victim.

Last week, I was confronted with such a moment. It began with a headache. Not an ordinary headache, but one of those soul destroying, "God, please let me die," headaches. Only this headache was not mine; it belonged to my ninety-year-old mother-in-law who was visiting us from two hundred miles away.

Like many of the elderly who are accustomed to living with daily pain, she tried to make light of it, saying, "Oh, it's nothing. I'm sure it will pass." But when she began shaking, and tears welled up at the corners of her eyes as she slowly made her way to the bedroom to "just lie down for a minute," we knew that this was something debilitating, and maybe even dangerous.

One watches the elderly like you watch an infant — with an unflagging and unceasing vigilance. And we did. As the night progressed, the headache became worse — disorienting, pounding. It was a sad and terrifying sight. At ninety, the body is so mortal, so thinly clothed in life — it seems like death is always a visitor standing quietly outside the door.

Her false teeth, her artificial eye, the hair she tints and keeps a rosy shade of chestnut — all these artifices of physical health and vibrancy were suddenly unimportant. She was a desperate and disheveled old woman, hanging onto a thread of life and clinging to us like a child clings to its parents.

My wife and I did the best we could, calling emergency wards, talking to on-call nurses, giving her pain medications that we thought her frail body could tolerate. But the situation only got worse. Finally, we had no choice but to bring her to the hospital.

Once in the emergency ward, all went well. She had the benefit of a young and caring woman doctor — exactly what she needed — and a few discoveries were made that argued for certain medications. We dutifully purchased the prescriptions and took her home for what we thought was going to be a gradual mending and returning to health.

But, after a day, the headaches returned, and this time with a vengeance. She was beside herself — a whimpering, injured animal unable to rest. She wandered frantically from room to room. She became confused and frightened. She would lie down for a minute, then get up again and start pacing. She couldn't eat; her voice was weak and wavering. She began talking about joining her deceased husband.

As this progressed into a second day, my wife and I knew that more had to be done. We again called the hospital for guidance. They told us to bring her to the clinic attached to the hospital for further assessment.

More tests were ordered. The staff did its best to make her feel comfortable. But the concern was real: this was a ninety-year-old woman who had always avoided doctors and had no relationship with any doctor at the clinic in her home town, and thus, no medical history to bring to bear on her condition other than the anecdotal information we children could provide. The doctors were starting from square one with a very ill patient who needed immediate treatment and intervention to ease her excruciating pain and, maybe, to save her life.

Meanwhile, our state was in the grip of a massive heatwave. The temperature at our house was well into the nineties; the city where my mother-in-law lives was crossing into the hundreds. Humidity was unbearable. People were suffering heat stroke, and the emergency wards in her home city were turning patients away because they had neither the staff nor the space to treat them.

It was against this backdrop that the doctors in our clinic made a discovery. My mother-in-law had a possible blockage of an artery that, left untreated, could lead within days to total blindness, stroke, and even death. The procedure required to confirm their diagnosis was surgical, but simple: a biopsy of a certain cranial artery.

Though she had other children who could arrange this at her home clinic if we were to get her back there, it became obvious that, under the circumstances, my mother-in-law couldn't travel. She needed to continue treatment at our clinic and hospital. We contacted her home clinic to ask for a referral so the costs of her treatment could be covered. We did everything according to her health plan's prescribed procedures — we amassed the proper notes, we contacted their office in a timely fashion.

We were not prepared for what confronted us. While a ninety-year-old woman, overwhelmed with terror and excruciating pain, sat awaiting approval for continued treatment, a referral person on the other end of the telephone line began interrogating us and questioning our motives. Was she really that sick? Why didn't we just bring her home?

We explained that she needed constant observation, and that her pain was so great that she could not easily make the four-and-a-half-hour trip through the uninhabited countryside in this sweltering heat. We were frightened for her well-being, and afraid of the possibility of an automotive breakdown in the debilitating heat.

The woman on the other end of the line was unfazed. "Don't you keep your cars in good repair?" she asked. "And why did you take her to the clinic rather than back to emergency?" Her manner was imperious; her questions phrased as accusations.

Through gritted teeth we tried to explain the realities of the trip, my mother-in-law's pain and frailty, and the way the clinic and hospital worked hand-in-hand where we live. The referral person at our clinic even got on the phone to explain the medical realities of the situation.

The woman listened impatiently, then announced, "If that were my mother, and I really cared about her, I would have gone back to emergency rather than waiting around for a clinic appointment. We will have to deny the referral."

My blood raced; my pulse pounded. I wanted to crawl through the phone and grab the woman by the throat. How could she, at that distance, make such a heartless decision? We had spent the night watching an elderly woman lying in bed, curled in a fetal position, shuddering with pain and fear, in possible jeopardy for her sight and even her life. Now this uninvolved administrator was demeaning us, and, ultimately, denying health care to that fragile, suffering woman.

"You're probably right," I snapped. "We should drive her down to your clinic. It will be far more cost effective for your health plan to treat a corpse, since they require only short office visits and seldom take up the doctor's time with small talk. Of course, they are notoriously slow to respond to treatment."

It was not my finest moment, but it made me feel better. The woman chuffed a few times, then repeated her administrative mantra. "We will have to deny the referral."

The referral person at our clinic was flummoxed. She tried in vain to convince the heartless gatekeeper on the other end of the line that this was a serious matter. But the woman from the distant clinic would not be moved.

As we got off the phone, our referral person said, "Go ahead. Take her in to our clinic. I'll stay on this one. We'll get this through." And so we left, and did what any caring children would do for a suffering parent. We simply went forward with treatment and figured, "Either treatment will be covered or it won't. We're not going to let someone we love suffer."

We left the grim cubicle where our referral person worked and returned to the clinic waiting room. We were worried and enraged. My mother-in-law was sitting alone — deaf, legally blind, in excruciating pain, and confused. Only a system that had sold its heart could deny such a person treatment. Claims of standards and cost containment and accepted administrative procedures meant nothing to us. We were looking into the face of a suffering human being, and, to us, any system that denied that poor woman treatment was an enemy.

But here is where a choice had to be made. We could remain in a rage, and spin downward into a fury against that health plan, health plans in general, the U.S. government, the ravages of age, a God who would allow such things, and anything else on which our free-floating anger might alight. Or we could affirm the good that had shown itself in the midst of the darkness swirling around us.

Twenty years ago I might have chosen the rage. It

would have been legitimate: good people everywhere are being ground to grit under these uncaring systems, and those who fight them are carrying the banner for everyone unable or unwilling to fight.

But there is a time for everything. Fighting the darkness does not increase the light, and I find that I too easily become what I'm fighting against. Better, at this stage of my life, to increase the light and leave the battles with darkness to others.

And so I left my wife and mother-in-law in the waiting room and went to the local florist and explained to the woman at the counter what had transpired and how valiantly the referral person at our clinic had worked on our behalf.

"Just a minute," the clerk said.

She went in back and came out with a beautiful flowering amaryllis. "This just came in," she said. "I was saving it for myself. But I want you to give it to that woman."

I looked at the plant. It was a cascade of delicate birthday-cake-pink flowers flowing forth from a succulent jungle of jade green leaves.

"This is perfect," I said. "She works in a basement. This will be a real splash of life and color in her life."

I took the flowering plant and went back to the clinic. My mother-in-law was now in the hands of a nurse, so my wife and I went down to the referral woman's office. She was sitting in her cubicle under the lifeless buzz of fluorescent lights. A computer screen was flickering in front of her and she was talking on a speaker phone to some insurance company's referral desk, trying to explain the need for a particular treatment for another patient. It was a reprise, though less urgent, of the conversation she'd had on our behalf the day before — one more thankless, frustrating conversation with a distant faceless administrator dedicated to weighing a patient's well-being against the cost of treatments.

When she got off the phone, we set the plant on her desk. The rich freshness of the green leaves and delicate flowers brought the dim institutional room alive. It seemed for all the world like a physical embodiment of the life and hope she had injected into our dealings with a gray and heartless system. She was genuinely overwhelmed.

"You didn't have to do this," she stammered.

"And you didn't have to do what you did for us," we responded.

And we were all right — none of us had to do what we did. But we had all reached further than we had to in order to make the system have a moment of heart. Our appreciation was genuine, and her appreciation was genuine. Together, we had infused some love and kindness into a situation where the only prior emotions had been anger and frustration.

We talked a bit more; then my wife and I went off to the clinic floor to be with my mother-in-law. We found her in the hands of a team of concerned doctors and nurses. Human compassion was asserting itself. We didn't yet have the outcome we all wanted, but we were in better spirits, knowing that good people were giving the best of themselves, and that in a·field of discontent, we had planted a tiny seed of goodness.

This may not seem like forgiveness, but in a very real though indirect way, it is. I could not, I would not — I did not wish to — forgive the health plan for so cavalierly jeopardizing the health and comfort of my elderly mother-in-law. Another person might have been able to take the long view, or to see the imperious woman's actions as just the misguided response of a person having a bad day. A better man might have been more understanding and, instead of lashing out, might have tried to neutralize her vitriol. But when I see suffering or callous indifference toward the weak by the powerful, my instinct is to fight for the weak rather than take the calmer, longer view, and for this I offer no apology.

But the real issue is not my response to the woman, but my response to the situation. Being unable and unwilling to forgive the system she was defending, and unable to dedicate my life to changing it, the only honorable course of action available to me was to increase the love and caring that had shown itself amid the indifference and frustration. And there had been many moments of caring: the referral woman in our clinic who tried so hard to help an elderly woman, the kind woman at the floral shop who had given up her plant for someone she had never met, the good and caring doctors, the concerned and helpful nurses, even my wife and I, at our better moments, as we stood up for the rights of an old woman who had given so much of herself to others for so many years.

Taken together, we were not equal in power to the grim architecture of the health plan. But we were its equal in heart. By forming a momentary network of caring, and acknowledging that caring, we tied ourselves together in a way that gave us each strength and sustenance. Human compassion was on our side, and compassion, if nurtured, will eventually win out over even the most inhumane structures.

Though we may not realize it, when we reaffirm the goodness that sprouts from the soil beneath the walls of hatred or indifference, we are practicing a kind of forgiveness, because we are saying that the hatred and indifference are not worthy of our anger. We are turning away from the great force of animosity, and underscoring, instead, the goodness struggling to find voice in its shadow. We may not be loving our enemy, but at least we are refusing to fight. We are asserting the light rather than engaging the darkness.

Jesus once said to his disciples, "If any one will not receive you or listen to your words, shake off the dust from your feet as you leave that house or town." There are times when it is better to walk away, not because the injustice should be ignored, but because there are houses where our kindness will be better received. In this instance, those houses were the hearts of the caring people who gave of their time and spirit.

I cannot say, in all honesty, that I think acts of kindness will bring a heartless system down. But there is some universal truth to the fact that when you withdraw energy from anything, it withers and dies.

I often think of the Berlin Wall. Who would have guessed that after twenty-eight years, that edifice, erected to form a barrier between philosophies and a wall between people, would come down almost without a struggle? It was as if it simply tired of supporting a negative, and gave way under the weight of its own gray spirit. Perhaps, with enough people planting seeds of caring around the wall of that health plan, it, too, will in time crumble and fall. It is surely fragile, for it lacks the mortar of love and caring.

But for me to join in battle with that health plan, at that particular moment, would have been fruitless. It would only have allowed the system to feed on my anger, which would have only made it stronger. By refusing to fight, perhaps I didn't make it weaker, but I made myself and those around me stronger.

When we are confronted with the machinery of indifference that is everywhere in our world, our best course may be simply to forgive ourselves for not being able to forgive, then go forward with the active forces of love and caring, however we can bring them to bear on the situation.

We can never underestimate the power of love, no matter how paltry, no matter how subversive. Much is going on in the shadows beneath dark and impenetrable walls. Sometimes, forgiveness is best served by planting flowers beneath those walls. We soon discover that others are down there with us planting flowers in the darkness.

When we are victims of faceless injustice, true forgiveness demands that we generate love.

Chapter 5

The Message Tree

❧

$\mathscr{I}$ am standing beneath a large and ancient cotton-wood tree in a shallow ravine in the far corner of northwestern Minnesota. A few feet in front of me a lazy flat-bottomed river meanders languidly between several low hillocks. The water is clear; I can see small fish moving between the shiny round rocks. On the far bank, maybe thirty yards away, a tangle of saplings and low, brushy undergrowth spreads out toward the base of the hillocks. To my right, patches of low meadow have formed in the oxbows where the river bends, and prairie birds trill and chirp from their perches in the tall grasses. Occasionally the splash of a redwinged blackbird cuts across my vision as it darts low over the meadow. Swarms of insects pool and buzz against the morning prairie light.

This is not a place many people would stop. The heavy stands of northern pines were left behind an hour ago, and the great expanses of rolling plains are still half a day's journey to the west. This is "get across" country — prairie flatness so great and empty that the full moon rising above it seems like the eye of God — solitary, singular, and all-seeing.

A few small towns pierce the horizon — tiny huddled settlements with French names like Huot and St. Hillaire, bespeaking the voyageurs who came here to trade with the Ojibwe Indians several centuries ago and ended up staying, either because they had taken Ojibwe wives, or because they had lost touch with the part of themselves that required civilization, and had replaced it with something wilder, more elemental, more irresistible.

I have always loved this great open country and these dying prairie towns. There is something peaceful and melancholy about them, like sad memories grown warm with age. They never really belonged here. The land was too harsh and unforgiving. For a generation or two they thrived — main street enclaves of two or three hundred people, set a dozen miles apart, each with its own church and school and hardware store and cafe. But now they are almost abandoned, and are left only to the few remaining store owners and old men in pickup trucks who gather daily at the local cafe to discuss the weather or the crops or the ills of a world that has stolen their children from them, leaving them to watch the town and the lives their fathers built dry up and blow away.

Despite the ceaseless labors of God-fearing hands, the deep winters and rocky soils mocked the efforts to create an agrarian lifestyle. These were lands better suited to yielding seasonal bounty to people passing through — people like the Ojibwe, who once called this land their own, and had it taken from them at the very site where I am standing, here on this still and lonely riverbank forty miles from the Canadian border.

I am listening closely. The singing of the leaves, the low murmur of the passing river, the flutter of birds, the buzz of the insects — all are part of a larger echo — an Ojibwe echo — and I can hear it in the wind.

I learned about this particular spot from an old man who died several years ago. I now come here whenever I am able to do honor to his memory. He was a hereditary Ojibwe chief. His grandfather had been part of a group of Ojibwe leaders who had come to this place in the fall of 1863. They had walked for days, leaving their home in the lakes and forests a hundred miles to the east, and making their way along the paths and riverways through this shapeless landscape that had been the hunting grounds of their people for generations. By the time they arrived here, the apple-sweet autumn breezes were starting to give way to the cold-edged winds of the looming northern winter.

The men had come to meet with representatives of the U.S. government. There had been some trouble between the Ojibwe and the white traders who traveled on the Red River oxcart trail between Winnipeg and St. Paul, and the government had insisted on this meeting.

There was a deeper purpose to their meeting, and the Ojibwe leaders were well aware of what was at stake. A year before, the same group of government soldiers and negotiators had been on their way up to this spot from the territorial capital in St. Paul, three hundred miles away, when trouble with the Dakotah Indians in the southern Minnesota Territory had caused them to detour south. The result of that detour had been a series of bloody battles, the forced exile of the Dakotah from their land, and the hanging of thirty-eight Indian men — the largest mass execution ever performed by the U.S. government. Some of the escaped Dakotah had come north to hide among the Ojibwe, and had told them of the slaughters to the south, so the Ojibwe now waiting on this riverbank were under no illusions about the intentions of the soldiers and negotiators they were about to meet. Whatever else they might claim the meeting was about, these men had been sent to take their land, and were going to do so by one means or another.

This site had been chosen for the rendezvous because of the cottonwood tree beneath which I am standing. It marks the best fording place on the river, and had been a message tree for as long as anyone could remember. The Indians had used it during their movements from the woodlands to the prairies, as had white traders and travelers who were making the five-hundred-mile journey across the prairie between the outposts of Winnipeg and St. Paul. Mail sacks were hung on its branches, messages were tacked to its bark. It had become a travelers' landmark in this otherwise featureless and windswept terrain.

There is a monument here — a strangely handsome bronze sculpture of an Indian man, standing like a Roman senator with a pipe in one hand and a cloak in the other. A few seldom-used picnic tables sit beside the dirt path that winds its way down the ravine to the river. But, other than that, there is only the wind, the low hills, and the quiet gurgle of the river as it meanders and oxbows between the brushy banks.

I look up at the great cottonwood. It is a giant, like all the cottonwoods that dot this landscape. Like the small towns that huddle on the prairie, these trees rise above the horizon line, offering landmarks for travelers and giving a sense of scale to the vast towering sky that vaults overhead. But unlike the towns, these cotton-woods have the stature to stand equal to the passing summer thunderheads and screaming winter winds that shape the seasons and the landscape. Unlike the towns, they seem to belong here.

The cottonwood's leaves are singing in the wind. Its high branches are swaying and dancing. The river is continuing its murmur, and far above me a hawk is riding the air currents, as if suspended in time and space. The whole setting seems suspended, as if in memory. It is easy to imagine the scene the old man had described to me when I used to visit him.

"Our people had camped in the meadow by the river," he told me. "The government troops were camped on the surrounding hills. Our people would come out of our tents in the morning, and all around us on the rises soldiers would be playing cards by their campfires with cannon and artillery aimed down on us."

The Ojibwe are a watchful people. They knew what the cannon meant, but they also knew what the scurry-ing animals and the chilling morning frosts meant. The steady drumbeat of an approaching winter was just over the horizon, and they knew that beneath the deliberate demeanor of the encamped soldiers was a growing fear of being trapped in this isolated and unforgiving land-scape, amid the howling winds and drifting snows of a shapeless six-month northern winter.

"Our people did not want to sell the land," the old man had told me. "We kept insisting on more time. The government negotiator, Alexander Ramsey, was getting angry. He kept telling us that we'd better agree soon. He kept reminding us of the trouble they'd had with the Dakotah down south and telling us we didn't want the same kind of problems."

I look at the low hills surrounding me. I imagine the tents, the soldiers, the artillery. I walk to the meadow where the old man said the Indians had camped. It is low and vulnerable, surrounded on all sides by the hills.

It is an eerie experience standing here alone on a waning summer day. I can sense the enclosure, the entrapment, the great noose closing around the necks of the Ojibwe as they discussed among themselves the words and the offers of this soldier who was telling them that they must give up the land they had sworn to their fathers and grandfathers to always protect.

It is easy to imagine the growing tension as, for weeks, the two groups gathered daily under this tree, the Ojibwe searching for a way to protect their land, the soldiers becoming increasingly nervous and irritable, while with each passing day the wind blew colder, the sky became more ominous, and the possibility of making it home for the winter became more and more remote.

Eventually, as the first frost tinged the prairie grasses and flocks of birds winged urgently overhead in their flight from the advancing winter, the government negotiators' patience ran out. It became inevitable that the Ojibwe had to sign and give away their land. Terms of compensation were determined, but those meant little to people who believed the land was their living mother. Under the threat of cannons, with full knowledge that their families would likely be massacred or exiled if an agreement was not reached, the Ojibwe leaders signed away the land where their ancestors were buried and which they believed that their God had granted them as an eternal and sacred trust.

As I stand here, all of this rushes over me. This is stolen land, part of a great historical tragedy. I think of the old man sitting in his chair, trying to communicate to me and a group of young Indian students the full tragedy of what they had lost at this spot. I hear his stories about the stern-faced priests and ministers who had ripped the children from their parents' arms — sometimes quite literally — and taken them, crying, to schools where they were made to disavow their gods and kneel on marbles with their arms out, balancing Bibles on either hand, if they were heard to speak a word of their own language.

I think of the elders I have known who were made to be ashamed of the fact that they grew up speaking their native tongue, and weep now as they look at their grandchildren and great-grandchildren left without moral moorings, drinking themselves to death and dying by their own hands.

How are these broken people to find a place of forgiveness in their hearts? How are they to look past an injustice that blows across the generations like the wind across this lonely prairie? It is easier to forgive crimes against ourselves than it is to forgive crimes against our children and grandchildren. These elders sit with a weight on their hearts that can never be lifted. But at whom are they to be angry? At all people of European descent, because we, somehow, in our color and origin, echo the people who stole the land from them and left them bereft of hope? At a government that acted on its best instincts of what it needed to do for its people, however misguided those instincts might have been? At a church locked into a vision of what God wanted for all people on this earth? At their own ancestors, for not fighting harder to protect the land they had no real choice but to sign away?

There is no honest target for the anguish that they feel. And yet the pain and rage are real, just as they were real for the old man as he sat in his chair, his body wasted by diseases brought to these shores by white immigrants, his heart broken by the rootlessness of the children he saw before him fidgeting and staring at the clock as he tried to communicate to them some sense of the birthright they had lost.

He showed us pictures of his grandfather — a regal and dignified man — and told us stories of the battles with the Sioux, and how his grandfather, wounded by arrows, had been brought back to his village on a travois. These stories were for him as real as the grandfather at whose knee he had been raised. But for me and the young Indian children they were as far away as King Arthur's round table or tales of the Arabian Nights.

How is he to forgive when the sorrow he feels is a pain with no source, when the injustice that leers at him is a grin with no face? How is the black father or the Hmong mother to forgive as they see their children descend into a hellish life of street violence and drugs, and know that though individual responsibility exists, their children's lives could have been otherwise had history not shown so cruel a hand?

This is the question that plagues me as I stand here on the bank of this forgotten river. How do you forgive a wrong when the wrongdoer is history, or a cultural mindset, or a season in the course of human affairs?

In such instances, where the source of the wrong is lost in the mists of history, the burden of forgiveness must fall on the hearts of those who endure that wrong.

There is no other choice. The elder in whose memory I stand here had every reason to feel outrage at the world that had destroyed his culture and betrayed the hopes of his grandchildren. But what good would that have served? There is no way to atone for what has been done, no restitution worthy of what he and his people have lost. How does one atone for a culture destroyed? How does one restore a heart long broken? We cannot turn back history and bring it to a different end, no matter how fervently we might dream that it could be so.

In such cases — when our spirits have been damaged by a wrong that has no face — we must try, as best as we are able, to transcend our grief and anger and look upon our lives as mirrors of universal laws. Life is growth, life is hope, life is change. To truly be part of life we must be part of hope and part of growth. Hatred in any form stands against growth and hope, because it stands against life. It corrodes the spirit like a disease wastes the body.

When some crime in the abstract has shriveled our soul into something hard and dark, then the goal of forgiveness should be to stand against the hate that the crime has engendered, and to restore our spirit — and the spirits of all others afflicted — to health.

We must remember that if there is nothing we can reasonably expect to forgive, there is nothing toward which we can reasonably direct our anger. If we hold onto that anger, it will eat at our heart and poison our spirit. And our anger will infect others, and move the world closer to a place of hatred than a place of love.

What we must do if we are the victims of faceless injustice is somehow find it within ourselves to generate love. This does not mean denying the wrong, or turning away from the truth. It means embodying, in our being, not only the truth of the injustice, but an attitude by which that injustice can be accepted, understood, and, ultimately, transcended.

The old man I have come here to honor knew this. In his mission to keep the memory of the past alive in young people, he also took it upon himself to show them a way to live with those memories.

All the great spirits of the world who have lived with injustice know this, and offer it to us in the example of their lives. Men like Nelson Mandela and Martin Luther King and Sitting Bull, women like Aung San Suu Kyi, know, in a way you and I never can, the scars of the oppression their people have suffered. But what makes them great, and a beacon for us all, is not their suffering, but the way they have chosen to respond to that suffering.

In some measure, greatness of spirit is achieved in proportion to the crime we are asked to forgive. Nelson Mandela, the Indian elder, all those who suffer greatly from the weight of faceless crimes, are great because of the generosity of heart required of them to live a life filled with compassion and love. But through a power of faith and will and a belief in the necessity of forgiveness, they live such lives.

I will never forget the words of Nelson Mandela, who, on the day of his release from prison after twenty-seven years of incarceration at the hands of the South African government, looked out upon the people who had gathered to hear him speak, and said, "Whites are fellow South Africans, and we want them to feel safe and know that we appreciate the contribution that they have made towards the development of this country."

He could have spoken in bitterness; he could have assumed an air of indifferent disdain. But he did not. He reached out to all around him, no matter what their color and history, and called them together as one.

He, like the old Ojibwe man, did not just model forgiveness, he embodied it. When Nelson Mandela walks down the streets of Capetown or Johannesburg, he shows those who shared his oppression how to live, and he lifts the heavy cloak of guilt from those who in the past were part of that oppression. He is a living testament to the wrongs of the past, but also an embodiment of the hope of the future.

If, as the Bible says, from those to whom much is given, much is expected, it is also true that for those to whom much harm has been done, much is possible. If it is our lot to live our lives under the shadow of a faceless crime, we should, as much as we are able, see ourselves as agents of redemption. For in us not only is the wrong embodied, but also the very forgiveness needed to restore the world to balance. The crime itself has disappeared; it is our responsibility to make the sense of guilt disappear.

All power of forgiveness is in the hands of those who have been wronged. If we are the inheritors of that wrong, we alone have the power to forgive. This is an awesome power.

As I stand here looking up at the cottonwood tree, I think once again of the old man who taught me about this place. He is now dead — gone to join the spirits of the negotiators, the soldiers, the tribal leaders, and the countless men and women, Indian and white, who have struggled on this hard land and have now begun to fade into history. But his vision remains alive in me, for he taught me lessons of forgiveness that only one who has been deeply wronged can teach.

He taught me that though I am not responsible, I must take responsibility. He showed me that I can feel a sense of obligation without feeling a sense of shame. He made me realize that not only can my hands help right the wrongs that others have caused, but that, indeed, they must.

By his gentle and steadfast witness, he both kept alive the wrongs of the past and pointed a way to their forgiveness in the future. Like this cottonwood tree, he was a beacon in a bleak and unforgiving landscape, an embodiment of strength and hope to all who passed. Like this tree, he showed us a way to cross the river that divides us.

From the greatest pain and sorrow,
a great forgiveness grows.

Chapter 6

Candles on the Grave

❧

$\mathscr{I}$t is near evening. The shadows are lengthening. The golden refracted light of day's end covers the world in a peaceful, radiant glow.

I am driving home, past the cemetery that sits in the middle of our town. Occasionally, when I drive by, a group of mourners will be standing around an open grave, and I feel that soft shudder of sadness that comes from brushing against a deep grief I cannot share.

Other times there will be bare-armed workers with shovels and front end loaders digging in the earth. Usually I look away. It is a strange sensation to be so near to death's immediacy, yet so far from its raw emotions.

But today something unusual catches my eye — a glint, a metallic flash, like a signal from a mirror. It seems a violation — an unseemly bit of transience amid the timeless granite headstones and restful, quiet greenery.

I drive around again, slowing at the point where the glint first caught my eye. It is still there, the same flash of movement, like light shimmering on sunlit waters.

Curious, I stop the car and step out. I'm not comfortable doing this, as I know no one in this cemetery. So I enter with a certain sense of apology, like a person walking into a house where he doesn't belong.

The glint of light continues, now joined by others. There is a rhythm to it all, a hurdy-gurdy lilt, floating on the currents of the wind. I walk closer. Banners, pinwheels, all manner of ribbons and tracery, float and dance on a small piece of ground. As I approach, I see that they are centered on a single grave.

As I get closer still, I see that the grave is covered with a hodgepodge of small toys — figures from fast food meals, miniature race cars, tiny trucks. Then, the photo — a framed school picture set upon the grave as if on a living room shelf. A young boy, maybe seven, maybe ten, smiling out at me, guileless, winning, full of hope.

A shudder runs through me. I think of my son, only ten himself, and retreat, filled with shame, to my car.

The next day, as I drive by again, I try to avert my

eyes. There is a knowledge here I don't want, a truth too horrible to absorb. Though my heart breaks at the tragedy of the small grave, it breaks at a distance, once removed from the immediacy of my own life. And that is how I wish it to stay.

But I can't help myself. The horror and fascination mingle, and like the sight of a fresh wound, I cannot keep my eyes away.

There it is again, the glint, the flash, the multi-colored motion. Even in the fading light it sings and dances against the somber stillness of the stones. But this time there is something more. On the grave, barely visible, I see a shadow. It is a woman, sitting, rocking gently. In her lap she holds a children's book. She is reading aloud to the grave.

My heart explodes. All around me cars are passing. People are hurrying home, planning supper, listening to traffic reports, running stoplights. What does this have to do with them, with me?

The voices of daily obligations swirl around me, garbled and grotesque. Stop at the grocery store. Don't forget the dry cleaning. Do the tires need rotating? Did Nick finish his homework?

But the voices sound flat and distant, like echoes from another world. All that is real to me is that silent shadow rocking in the distance. And that shadow no longer cares if her boy finishes his homework. She no longer cares about supper, about tires, about anything at all. She is sitting among the toys that once littered her living room floor, reading a children's book to a grave. I want to approach her, to try to console her, to tell her that I stand in silent witness to her sorrow. But what would that matter? I am from the land of the living. She wanders in the fields of the dead.

My spirit arches, out of control. What kind of world is this that takes a child from its mother? What sort of God condones these tragedies, then asks us to make sense of them? There is no rationale or justification. To say that this is part of some divine plan, unfolding before us and through us toward an unknowable wisdom, is like dry dust to that mother reading to the grave. Does God think us so docile that we should be satisfied with saying, "All people must die. There is a reason beyond our knowing"?

I have listened to preachers, standing over small coffins, fumbling for words and trying to shape meaning from tragedy. They invoke the unknown, praise the unknowable, speak of better lives, of lessons for the living. But their explanations are all empty, like husks rattling in the wind. When they have finished with their words, the dark truth still remains, and we can do no more than bow our heads before the mystery, and sit in silent grief until the balm of time reduces our pain to a burden we can bear. For such grieving we need no preachers. We need only the patience of the wounded, and such patience is given to the believer and the doubter alike.

But I am weary of patience. I want more as I look at this woman. I want more for her, and for me. I want God to step out from behind the veil of inscrutability and offer explanation. I want God to give me a reason. I want God to apologize.

"Why did you take that child from that mother?" I want to ask. "Why do you set her apart for all time from a moment of pure peace in her heart? If I were God, there would be no such crimes against the innocent. Good people would be rewarded. Bad people would be punished or changed. I would not sit at some haughty distance, toying with people like so many insects. We do not deserve this. This is the work of a bully God, and I do not choose to see you as a bully."

But God is silent, and the silence feels like mockery.

"Why do you do these things?" I continue. "What possible good can there be in taking a child out of season? Have you not set rules, and placed them in nature, that a child cannot be born before the parent? Then why have you not set rules that say that the child cannot be taken before the parent? Are you so indifferent to the fragile spirit that dwells within us that you cannot see that you have frozen the heart of this mother for all time? If you will not apologize, can you not at least explain?"

But there is no answer. Only the wind blowing

through the gravestones, and the shadow reading silently to the grave.

The light changes. The cars proceed. I hurry home to open envelopes and place pennies in a jar.

The next day, again, I drive past. And the day after that. Sometimes the woman is there, sometimes she isn't. The decorations on the grave change, like the toys on the shelf in a child's bedroom. One week there is a large sunflower amidst the profusion of tiny plastic figures. The next there is a collection of stuffed animals.

On rainy days it all becomes sodden, and seems to sink toward the ground in despair. On bright, windy days, it all glistens and dances and swirls, as if in celebration. Gradually, this tragic shrine is becoming part of my life.

But still, I feel dishonest, like a man peering in the window on another's grief. I owe the woman who lives with this grief the honor of telling her that I, too, am moved by their tragedy, if only at a distance. The next time I see her, I resolve to stop.

On the following Tuesday afternoon she is there. She has placed a low white garden fence around the grave's perimeter, and she is spreading a fresh blanket of rich, thick, black dirt over the ground with a rake. All the toys and animals have been moved back against the fence, where they sit, in waiting, like guests at a party.

I approach cautiously, almost apologetically.

"Excuse me, " I say. "I don't want to bother you.

But sometimes I stop here. Can I ask you about your child?"

She looks at me and smiles. "They don't care about the graves," she says. "They never pick the weeds." She doesn't stop her raking.

"Will you tell me about him?" I ask.

She pulls the rake across the fresh dirt, making sure the new seed she has planted is spread evenly across the ground.

She glances at me for a moment. "He was a good boy. When we took him to the nursing home to visit his great-grandmother, we walked in the door and his eyes got wide. 'Oh, look at all the grandmas and grandpas I have,' he said." Her raking never stops.

"He sounds like a special child," I say.

"He is," she answers.

I kneel down and look at the photo. His face is winning, full of innocence and hope. She pauses for a moment to watch me watch him.

"He loved everyone," she says. "One time there was an ant hill in front of the house. I had the broom and was going to sweep it away. He stopped me. 'No, those are my friends,' he said. That's what he told me: 'Those are my friends.'"

Her memories are specific — exact moments, full of detail and life. In each of them, the child speaks.

"Are these his toys?" I ask, looking around at the audience of stuffed animals and plastic figures. She nods.

Tears are beginning to well up in her eyes. She points to a little plastic bug that sits in vigil on the top of the fence. "That bug is because he was my little love bug," she says.

She picks up a little lantern. Its top is covered with tinfoil to keep the wind out. "I light a candle for him every night, because he was the light of my life," she says.

The words are coming harder now. She looks around at the expanse of silent stones and quiet greenery. "I wish I could put a candle on every grave," she says, "so all these people would be remembered. There are so many. So many . . ."

Her voice trails off. She is moving inside herself, moment by moment. It is time for me to go.

"Thank you for sharing him with me," I say. It sounds stupid, clumsy. But she does not seem to mind.

I turn to leave, feeling like an intruder. She stops me with her voice.

"Do you have a child?" she asks.

I turn back toward her. "Yes," I answer, almost ashamed. "A boy, ten."

She pulls the rake gently across the grave. "Hug him," she says. "You go home and hug him."

I walk back toward my car, full of unfathomable grief and gratitude. Behind me, I can hear the rough scratching of the rake on the earth.

If there is a challenge in the great tragedies that

are visited upon us, it is only this: that if we were not to transcend them, we would descend into a darkness so great that, like a star burning in upon itself, we would implode, taking all with us as we died.

We cannot let this happen. Even in the face of death and inexplicable tragedy, we must persevere, walking in zombie steps toward some light we cannot see. For from great darknesses either bitterness or mercy grows — a bitterness that it had to be so, and that it happened to us, or a mercy for all else in life that reminds us of what we have lost.

We must choose mercy; it is our only course. Though its cause may be dark, and though we may not sense it at the time, it makes us a vessel of grace. It fills us with unbounded love that pours forth without judgment on all it sees, because it knows that every life, no matter how flawed or humble, is precious beyond measure, and that even the briefest moment of life deserves to be held aloft and offered up to God.

As I walk away from the grave, I think of that young mother and the burden she carries. For years, and, in some measure, for her entire life, when she sees children at play, she will see only the ghostly echo of her own fallen child. But then, so slowly, that echo will animate her love for those other children in a way that she never would have known had her own child lived to become the vessel to receive all her love.

Like a priest giving himself to God, or a God giving

himself to all humanity, she will give herself to all children, without question or reserve, wherever she meets them in the course of life. Perhaps behind her eyes others will see the dark hurt that will never be erased. But in those eyes they will also see the love that now spills over, unable to be contained, on all children who echo the memory of her fallen child.

The gift she has received — the darkest of gifts — is that she no longer gives forgiveness, she now is forgiveness, and no crime that any living child may commit will ever cause her to withdraw her love from that child. And no child, however forlorn, will ever be in her presence again and not feel the overwhelming mother love, flowing, as strong as an ocean current, toward them.

In her all children's sins have died forever. Through the many sorrowful years remaining in her life, she will become the pure light of mother's love, and in her eyes the rest of us will learn, if only dimly, the value of that which we hold so fragile in our hands.

Through her grief and sorrow, she will become the perfect forgiveness we long to feel in our own hearts. She has been crucified for all motherhood, and has taken our sins upon her.

I turn to see her one more time. She is bending down and lighting the lantern. She is whispering, or singing.

I cross myself — an almost involuntary act from my distant past.

Upon her shoulders is the burden of all loss. But in her heart a candle burns for every child, and in her presence, every child will forever be embraced and welcomed home.

Forgiveness is simply love put into action.

Chapter 7

Poisoned Waters

❧

Do not avoid contact with suffering or close your
eyes before suffering. . . . Suffering nourishes compassion.
— Thich Nhat Hanh

$\mathcal{I}$ am sitting on an overlook above Prince William Sound on the Kenai Peninsula in southeastern Alaska, watching the gentle closing of the day.

It is hard to imagine a setting of greater beauty, or one more alive with the symphony of life. Mountains stretch from horizon to horizon, and recede into the distant mists. Glaciers fill the crevasses and probe like fingers toward the sea. Seabirds circle among the clouds, screeching and keening. The wind whispers with the ancient breath of the great descending ice fields, and, far below, on the surface of the sound, the rhythmic wash of the restless waters catches the cadence of my heartbeat, and holds it.

I have come here with my son, who is asleep beside me. I would like to wake him so we could share this moment. But his days are full, and his sleep is deep. I leave him to his dreams and face this majesty alone.

Though it is almost ten o'clock, twilight is just beginning to creep across the land. The shadows are lambent. The alpenglow is turning the distant peaks to fire. The sky, so insistent on holding its light, is suffused with a purple cast. Soon the darkness will rise up from within, and the colors of the day will fade, leaving only the quiet immensity of night. I stand humbled, awestruck, honored to witness this slow turning of the spheres.

But another thought humbles me as I look out over this scene of almost transcendent beauty, and it does not humble me with joy, but with sadness. The lapping waters and shoreland beaches far below me are the waters and shores that not so many years ago were blanketed with the great oil spill from the ruptured tanker *Exxon Valdez*.

I had heard about the spill, maybe had shaken my head at the pointlessness and wanton ecological brutality of it. But it had touched only my mind, and not my heart.

But that all changed this afternoon. My son and I came across an exhibition housed in a small cinderblock building in the coastal town of Seward. It was dedicated to explaining the oil spill and its ecological effects. The exhibition, sponsored by the University of

Alaska at Fairbanks, was unassuming, even amateurish. It consisted of display tables with objects related to the oil spill and cleanup efforts, a series of photographs and recordings, and various science project–level graphs and maps that tried to put the catastrophe into a manageable scale. But, despite its humble presentation — and, maybe, because of it — it succeeded.

To see the photographs of harbor seals' desperate eyes as they tried to clean the oil from their pelts, or the bodies of seabirds contorted in agony, and to multiply it by the magnificent scale of this landscape; to read the words of the Native woman who walked out of her door that morning and, for the first time in her life, heard only silence, and to imagine that against the raucous music of nature that surrounds me now; to see the pitiful rags and mops and five-gallon buckets that people used to try to clean up a spill that stretched the equivalent distance from Portland to San Francisco; to stare into the oil-splattered faces of the men and women who ran from their homes with towels and blankets and tried to clean off the sea otters and birds and sea life that were writhing and flopping in death agonies on the beach — these images filled me with a deep and unassuageable grief.

But at the end of the exhibit was something that troubled me almost as much as the exhibition itself. A notebook was displayed in which people had written their responses to the exhibit and the spill. Most people were touched deeply by the cataclysm. Some were shamed, some were enraged, some took the position that this disaster was the price we must be willing to pay if Alaska is to build its prosperity on so fragile and potentially lethal an industry as oil. But almost no one was unmoved, one way or the other, and they made their various points of view known with passion and conviction.

But there was one comment that took a different tack. In a gracious and elegant script that spoke of intelligence and education, a woman had written, "No more name calling and finger pointing. It is as destructive as an oil spill."

I thought of the anguished faces of those exhausted workers, close to tears from the hopelessness of their task. I thought of the cylinder of crystallized oil that had been scooped up from between the rocks a decade after the spill, and of the thousands of tons of similar material that are congealed on the bottoms of rocks throughout the sound, slowly leaking their toxins into the sea for centuries to come. I thought of the species that have not yet recovered, and may never recover. And I wanted to tell that woman, "No. You are wrong. Finger pointing and name calling are not as destructive as an oil spill. If all the people from Portland to San Francisco wake up one day and find themselves face to face with a spreading shroud of death that has killed all small creatures in its wake, then that is as destructive as an oil spill. If people take up arms, kill species, and destroy their habitats so that they cannot recover, then that is as destructive as an oil spill. But the raw human emotions of grief and outrage at this senseless destruction of life are not as destructive as an oil spill. They may not be pretty, they may not be the highest expression of the human spirit. But they are not as destructive as an oil spill."

But this woman would not have heard me. She had decided that negative emotions were more destructive than negative events, and had chosen to turn her eye away from a harsh and tragic reality, reducing it to a clean, more easily resolved issue of personal growth and consciousness.

I was reminded of an event that had occurred years ago in a class I was teaching at a local college. I had shown the students a haunting documentary in which the filmmaker had chronicled the reminiscences of people whose lives had been touched by the Holocaust. He had made no overt moral judgments. He had talked to whomever he could find — Nazi commandants who had been entrusted with the task of finding efficient ways to kill people without wasting bullets, peasants who had watched the trains full of

Jews roll past their small Austrian villages, the loco-
motive engineers who had driven those trains, the victims themselves who had lived through the misery and
horror of the death camps — no one who had witnessed
that period of history had escaped the filmmaker's
gaze.

It was a mesmerizing film, made all the more rivet-
ing because the filmmaker let the people tell their own
stories. He offered no commentary, showed no grainy
filmclips of bulldozed piles of bodies. Instead, he let
the horror pile up, moment by moment, through the
accretion of ordinary detail. After a while, its cumula-
tive effect became almost unbearable.

At the end of the class, one of the students, a
woman in her thirties, came to me, visibly upset. "How
dare you make me watch something like that," she
said. "I'm not here to have negative thoughts shoved
down my throat. I don't need to fill my mind with these
kinds of things." Then she stalked out.

In her own way, she was no different from the
woman who had written the note in the log book here in
Alaska. In both cases, it was not the cruelty of the circumstances, the incalculable suffering and destruction
of life that upset them, it was dwelling on the reality of
that suffering and destruction. What they saw was not a
betrayal of our responsibility to the fragile and inter-
connected web of life, but a betrayal of their belief in

the power of positive thought, and their commitment to always looking on the bright side, seeing the glass as half full, finding a silver lining.

We Americans are a unique breed. We are raised to believe that optimism is a virtue, not simply a point of view. Looking at the darkness in human affairs is seen as spiritually retrograde, deficient in some fundamental characteristic of optimism that we are taught to believe is the engine of spiritual betterment in the universe. Why muck about in the regions of suffering and hatred when we could as easily, and much more fruitfully, use our consciousness to move toward a vision of the light?

This is the position that both women had taken. They had reduced something irreducible in human affairs to an issue the size of their own personal consciousness, and they found people's response to the event to be more significant than the actual event itself.

But some events are larger and more far reaching than an individual human consciousness. An oil spill that shrouds an entire coastline in death; a Holocaust that allows six million innocent people to be systematically exterminated — these are events where ignoring the dark side and focusing on the positive is not an act of forgiveness, but a betrayal of our human responsibility as stewards of the earth and a denial of our brotherhood and sisterhood with all other living beings.

In such instances, forgiveness must take a different shape. It must begin with an acknowledgment of the darkness in human affairs, and work to bring light into that darkness. Perhaps that acknowledgment involves anguish, sadness, even something akin to despair. Perhaps it involves accepting a level of personal anger that comes close to emotional violence. There is no shame in feeling these emotions — they are the human, and very legitimate, responses to unspeakable crimes and violations of the human spirit. The only shame is in embracing these emotions and using them to justify acts of retribution and vengeance. The forgiving heart, though it may feel these emotions, seeks a way to transform them into positive action, and to rise from the darkness into the light.

This is a hard truth about forgiveness. It often must begin in anger and sadness, because it begins with the discovery that some fundamental human trust has been betrayed. The heart naturally recoils at this discovery, and is flooded with dark emotions. Yet it must overcome these emotions, and rise toward the light. If, in its desire to avoid these emotions, it turns away from the events that cause them, it is not acting with forgiveness, it is acting in denial.

We must learn to recognize the difference between letting go of hurts and standing up against wrongs. All of us experience hurts in our lives. The forgiving heart knows that it must turn the other cheek on these hurts, even if they wound us deeply. But the forgiving heart also knows that when wanton acts of violence are committed against the innocent, or acts of callous indifference are visited upon the weak by the powerful, we become complicit in the injustices of the world by accentuating the positive or "putting it all behind us." In such cases, a forgiveness based in looking past the wrong is no forgiveness at all, but an act of moral blindness and even cowardice. It is to confuse forgiving with forgetting, and there are some instances where forgiveness requires not that we forget, but that we remember.

The sad truth is that hatred is real. Cruelty is real. Injustices against the innocent are real. Whether we like it or not, we are not fully human unless we acknowledge the dark side — of the world, of human potential, of our own personalities. Harsh though it sounds, we live a lie if we stare only at the good, and worst of all, if we shutter our own awareness, we allow the darkness in the world to move unchallenged over the landscape, savaging the innocent and feeding upon the helpless.

What the forgiving heart must do is wade into the darkness, knowing that against the light of goodness, darkness cannot stand. It must recognize the darkness, but act toward the light. Those weary and heartbroken workers, scrubbing the oil from the terrified birds and sea otters and harbor seals, may have been fighting back tears and uncontrollable anger as they worked. But their act was one of forgiveness, because it was an act of hope.

The people who stood against the Nazi atrocities after the war and choked back their own outrage as they labored for justice rather than revenge were working toward forgiveness far more surely than those who turned away from the atrocities because they refused to focus on the negative.

Sometimes we arrive at forgiveness only by the hard labors of our heart. In both these cases, what made their acts forgiving was their commitment to life rather than death, their belief that we must stand up for love, even in the face of unrelenting cruelty and hate.

When Jesus drove the moneychangers from the temple, he acted not out of a hatred for the money changers, but from a love for the sacredness of the temple. In the same way, cries of anguish at the crimes committed against this beautiful land by the oil spill are not necessarily statements of hatred toward those who caused that spill as they are testaments of love for the beauty and sacredness of the landscape and the life that was despoiled.

This, it seems to me, is the key to honest forgiveness. When our actions are based in love and a belief in the sanctity of all life, they are actions of forgiveness. When they are based in hate, they are actions of vengeance. And actions of vengeance poison the waters of the heart as surely as the oil spill poisoned the waters of this sound.

I think of that now as the sun goes down in a final blaze of lavender and magenta over this majestic landscape, so beautiful, so damaged, so revealing of the hopes and failures of the human heart. And as I listen to the rhythmic breathing of my sleeping son, and measure it against the distant lapping of the wounded waters, I know in my heart where true forgiveness lies for me.

It is not in turning away from anger, or denying my outrage at the wrongs and indignities of life. It is in rising each morning and going forth into the oil spills of life, with buckets and mops and rags of hope, trying to create a better world for our children.

If my eyes are filled with tears, it does not matter. Those tears will dry. But if I act from faith and love, and not from hatred and vengeance, the legacy of my hope, and the memory of my efforts, will pass down to my children, and my children's children, and buoy them with the sense of possibility that I carried in my heart.

I think of a story I once heard told by a relief worker in West Africa during one of the terrible, killing droughts that left thousands dying of thirst and starvation. He had been sent to one of the refugee camps where people were supposed to come for food and medical assistance. It was like a sea of humanity, he said. People sitting, lying down, staring with eyes almost devoid of light. And silent — eerily and deathly silent. He would walk among the emaciated bodies, and as he passed, the faces would stare up at him with empty eyes that betrayed no emotion. Here and there a baby's cry could be heard; then the shroud of silence would return.

It was beyond hope and despair, he said. It was simply horror. A scream with no sound. Mothers holding dead infants. Children lying next to their dead parents. A mass of humanity, dying and dead, spread out across the sweltering, waterless plain, covered with dust and flies, not moving, just staring.

The workers would bring food among them and hand it to those still able to eat — bowls of gruel, sips of water. But in the face of the sea of death and suffering, it was as nothing.

One day, he saw a man crawling. It was intentional and purposeful, unlike the random, aimless stumblings he was accustomed to seeing from the dying. The man had a small bowl of gruel. He was pulling himself along on skeletal arms, stopping before each of the nearby children and putting a bit of the gruel on their lips. The relief worker watched in horror and fascination. "I felt like I was watching a saint," he said.

The next day, the man was dead.

That image has forever stayed in my mind. That was true forgiveness. It did not despair, it did not turn away. In its own small way it was an act of hope — at once an act of defiance and an act of affirmation. Far more than anyone turning away from the horror to look at the good in life, this was an assertion of the positive, a statement that we live to serve, and that we are all connected by the touches we make with each other. It was not an attempt to see good, it was an attempt to create good.

Was there any anger or outrage left in that man? I don't know. Did he have a sense that this universe was unjust, and that any God that existed must either be indifferent, or mocking and jeering? I don't know. Did he hate the well-fed white faces who for years had ignored the wars and famines of his people, and now, too late, brought water and gruel to his starving brothers and sisters who lay dying on that parched ground? Who is to say?

None of that really matters. What matters is that he acted with charity and hope, and with the belief in the sanctity of all life, no matter how fleeting or humble. He took his ragged shred of life and reached out from it with love to those he could touch with his hands. And in that moment of placing the food on the starving child's lips, he gave more of himself, and gave more to the sense of justice and forgiveness in this world than I may in all the days I live.

I often think of Jesus, praying in the Garden of Gesthemane, uttering the cry, "Father, if it be possible, let this cup pass from me."

We do not always get to choose the cup that is handed us. Sometimes we would rather let it pass. But the choice is not ours. We must willingly accept the cup that is given us, raise it up, and consecrate it with the faith that our actions may turn it into something holy and life affirming. They may not; but that is not ours to say. That African man surely did not save the lives of those children whose lips he blessed with that touch of water and food. Those weary and heartbroken workers, scrubbing the oil from the terrified birds and sea otters and harbor seals, may, in the last analysis, have saved nothing at all.

But their act was one of forgiveness, because it was an act of hope and affirmation, and no less so if it was performed with an angry or anguished heart. We become what we do, and if we act with forgiveness, we become forgiveness, and, in some way we will never understand, we add a thread of light to the fabric of this vast and confusing universe.

The Lakota people say that we must live our lives

and make our decisions with an eye to the seventh generation. Honest forgiveness must have this vision at its heart. The healing of the self; the removal of personal tension and conflict; the calming of the heart — all of these are worthy goals, because they help restore the spirit to the equilibrium necessary to act with clarity. But if this calming and clarifying of the spirit is achieved at the expense of an honest appraisal of the world around us, and is not based on restoring the world — not just ourselves — to a state of health, it is not an exercise in spiritual growth, but an act of spiritual delusion. It makes our pursuit of individual spiritual growth a tinkling cymbal and sounding brass, and reduces it to nothing more than an exercise in personal psychology.

I look now at my son, sleeping next to me. And I listen to the distant lapping of the wounded waters and the screeching cries of the seabirds who now may carry death in their very blood and bones. In my mind I see the thousands of starving African eyes staring at me, and deep in my heart I hear the ghostly footsteps of the six million souls who perished in a madman's ovens. And these things make me sad and angry and ashamed.

But they do not take the forgiveness from my heart. My forgiveness is that I raise this child who now sleeps so innocently beside me with a knowledge that, for all the darkness in this world, there are still people who will wash oil from the wings of dying seabirds and place food on the parched lips of starving children. And that he, as someone blessed to have received the miraculous gift of life, must learn, in his own time and circumstances, to take his place among them.

I cannot say what cup will be handed him, whether his life will be easy or hard, whether it will be blessed with good fortune, or visited with tragedy and hardship. But I can teach him to consecrate whatever cup he is given, and to hand it on to the next generation with a sense of possibility and hope.

We are, each of us, God's hands here on earth. If we turn away from the darkness, the light of goodness and hope will fade in the very places it is most needed. We must not let this happen. We must, as much as we are able, strive to live our lives as stewards of the earth. We are our brothers' and sisters' keepers, and where our brothers and sisters live in darkness, it is our obligation to bring the promise of a healing light.

This is what I want my sleeping child to learn from this beautiful and tragic setting. I want him to find in himself the courage to cry in outrage at the dying seabirds even as he learns to stand in awe at the overwhelming beauty of the landscape. I want him to learn that though it was the hand of God that created this land, it is his hand that can save it. I want him to learn to measure his heart not by his anger, or his own well being, or some personal sense of self-betterment based in asserting the positive, but by his commitment to preparing a better earth for those who are yet unborn.

If he can learn these things, he will be a forgiving person, because he will have the courage to stare with full awareness at the cruelty and injustice in the world, yet say with honesty, "I will not be swallowed up by the darkness, but will go forward with hope and compassion not seven times, but seventy times seven times."

He will understand that forgiveness is simply love put into action, and that, in some way he can never comprehend, cleaning oil from the feathers of a dying seabird will allow some child seven generations hence to wake to a moment of sunshine, and greet the day with delight and laughter rather than with the hollow eyes of hunger and despair.

Far below me now, the waters have disappeared into darkness. They heave and mingle with the breathing of my child. In the growing night the seabirds scream, and on my lips I feel a distant thirst.

We are all connected in ways we will never understand. What is done to the least of us is done to us all.

I reach down and touch the face of my sleeping son. The world is filled with possibilities beyond our imaginings.

*Forgiveness is a wind from the heart
of God, and we must let it take
us where it would have us go.*

Chapter 8

An Embrace of the Heart

It is October, now. A fresh breeze is blowing through the autumn pines. With their timeless knowledge, they know that winter is coming, and it makes them soft.

It makes me soft, too, amid the hard edges of my days. It humbles me, quiets me, reminds me that life is great and I am small.

I want to embrace this autumn wind. It is so much of what I long to be — warm, calm, a little winsome for what we have lost, but full of confidence and hope. It is a wind of forgiveness that carries no bitterness, no anger for the passing of the season, only knowledge that this is how things must be, and a faith, almost to the point of knowing, that warmth will come again.

But I cannot embrace a wind; I can only give myself over to it, and let it take me, like a leaf, where it would have me go.

Perhaps that is what I — we — must learn of forgiveness — that it is a wind from the heart of God, a faith to the point of knowing that goodness will prevail, and that we must let it embrace us, and lift us, and take us where it would have us go.

The greatest among us rise on this wind, and cause the rest of us to look upward toward the stars. But we, the ordinary, blown through the brambles of daily frustrations and irritations and grievances against God and man, move a bit, then get tangled again, never rising, never lifting, aware more of the snares that entangle us than the wind that moves us. But the wind is there, like a constant melody, and it is ours to hear if only we open our hearts to its song.

Yesterday I sat at a children's playground. I closed my eyes and listened to the laughter, the arguments, the whole cacophony of innocent music, so abundant, so confusing, but always so full of life and hope. How could I not believe in forgiveness at such a moment, knowing that in every town, in every language, everywhere on earth, in every generation, the same music can be heard?

And how could I not believe that an honest forgiveness must seek first and always to protect that music, and to keep alive in these children the possibility of love?

That is what this wind commands of me — that I hear its music everywhere I am, and I add to its voice in any way I can.

Perhaps I wash a dying seabird, trying to give it a moment's peace in its oily death. Who am I to say that it cannot feel the power of my sorrow and my love?

Perhaps I bring a gift to someone in defiance of my anger. Is this not a hallowing of the wind amidst the brambles of my rage?

Perhaps I listen in caring silence while a friend pours forth his anguish at his human weakness, then offer him the forgiveness of a smile. Perhaps I stand, resilient, in witness to a faceless wrong, and show the children, by my witness, how to live. Perhaps I light a candle for my grief, and let that grief pour forth from me until, consecrated by the healing hand of time, it turns to love. Perhaps I do nothing but revisit the story of my life, painting my memories in colors of humility and gratitude.

How I listen to this wind is mine alone to decide. But if I listen with a pure heart, and allow it to blow gently into the corners of my life, it will embrace me and lift me and move me in ways I cannot imagine.

As I sit now, beneath this gentle swaying pine, two memories float before me. The first is of a time I spent in the home of a friend in a city far from my own. His young son had just turned seven months. The child's eyes were still wide with discovery, and his every glance celebrated the mystery of life.

Much to my delight, the child took an immediate

liking to me. Whenever I entered the room, he would stare at me with light in his eyes and hold out his pudgy arms, waiting for me to lift him and hold him. I would go to him and pick him up, basking in the joy of a fresh life, new upon this earth, that saw in me something it could trust, and toward which it could direct its unprotected spirit. I held him with a sense of reverence and joy.

Though my days were occupied with what were supposed to be more important matters, what I most savored during my trip was returning to my friend's house and picking up that guileless, trusting child who eagerly held out his young arms and waited for my embrace.

I would cradle him in my arms; he would grasp me tightly. We would stand together, a man in the full strength and awareness of midlife, and a child in the dawning of his days, sharing a warmth and a trust that overcame all differences of biology and chronology, and made us, for a moment, two people with a common heart.

The second event took place several months later. I went to visit an elderly aunt who lay dying in a hospice. We had always cared about each other but had never spent much time together. As a child, I would see her several times a year at family gatherings, then would run off to play with the other children. As an adult, I had visited her on numerous occasions, but always as a courtesy call on someone who had been good to me and who I knew would gain pleasure from my visit. We had cared about each other, but there had been no deep sharing of the intimacies of each other's lives.

But on her deathbed, something changed. When I came to visit her, we found ourselves inexplicably drawn to each other. Who I was at the moment, and the questions that concerned me in life, seemed to fit exactly with her needs for self-examination at the time of her dying.

She craved my presence, and I, hers. I would sit by her bedside, holding her hand, telling her what I knew about different religions' beliefs about death, asking her about the uncharted landscape she was exploring moment by moment, and simply being present to the mysterious power of her dying.

As I left her the last time — and we knew it was the last time, for my home was hundreds of miles away and I had no plans to return for months — we simply held each other. There was no other way to seal what we had been sharing. Then, like ships setting out to sea, we let each other go and passed, for all times, from each other's sight.

Neither of these events was momentous. They were the common clay of everyday life. But, each, in its own way, spoke the same fundamental truth. Here I was, at the peak of my powers in life, having been blessed with the opportunity to be present to two people — one at the beginning of life, one at the end of the journey — who were physically helpless but spiritually guileless and pure of heart. And, in each case, what they sought most from me, and I from them, was to be held. Anything else we would have shared would not have meant as much.

What more do I need to know about forgiveness? It is an embrace, across all barriers, against all odds, in defiance of all that is mean and petty and vindictive and cruel in this life. It is a wind blowing warm through the cold regions of our heart, embracing us all, and lifting us in hope and promise toward a vision of what we might yet become.

We live in a time that values the harder virtues — self-reliance, the ability to stand up for oneself, the capacity to speak one's mind with honesty and clarity. We equate power with the ability to dominate, and success with the capacity to win. The gentler virtues, like forgiveness, that speak in a quiet voice, are barely heard. But it is in the gentler virtues that true strength lies.

When I stood there, looking into the eyes of that child just coming into life, and at a woman on the verge of leaving it, all else was stripped away — all the intellectual pretense, all the analysis, all the words; all the issues of dominance, success, self-reliance, and achievement were nothing. The strongest act, the redemptive act

— the only act — was the gentlest act of being willing to hold and be held.

This is what the forgiving heart knows, and this is how it calls us to live. Embrace, it says. Embrace the child with whom you are angry. Embrace your husband or wife, with whom harsh words have passed. Embrace the parents who gave you life. Embrace the world that confuses you and the God that confounds you.

And embrace yourself, in all your flaws and hopes and weaknesses and dreams. Embrace them all, like the wind embraces you. Embrace them, and lift them, and consecrate them with hope.

We are ordinary people, walking a difficult path through a vast and confusing universe. Despite our best intentions, we all slip, stumble, and fall. There is not one among us who does not, in the dark of some private night, wish to have at least one moment back, one step to make again. But time moves forward, and takes us in its tide.

I think now of my father, gently opening my bedroom door and quietly asking if I wanted to go with him to a fire or a drowning. Did he think that in those moments he would be shaping me in a way that I would struggle all my life to understand? I think of my son, and the touches, so well meaning, that I make upon his life. Will he not also be shaped in ways I cannot imagine?

Was it so different for the missionaries who, in their

zeal for their god, crushed the spirits of the native people they had gone to serve? Or for my mother's father, as he struggled vainly to stumble home from some corner bar with some small gift for his daughters, only to fall asleep on a neighbor's lawn, and have to be carried home in shame by those he only sought to love?

We see through a glass darkly, and none of us more clearly than the rest. All we can do is embrace the world that is given us, knowing that it is in our hands alone to shape the moments through which we pass. If we shape them poorly, we need not be ashamed, so long as our heart is pure and our hands are caring. The wind of forgiveness blows through our lives, too, and it is beyond our vision to say which touches will harm and which will heal.

But this much we can know. It is in the eyes of the children that the truth will be known. If our actions fill the eyes of the children with love, they are actions of forgiveness. If they fill them with fear and sorrow, no claim we make for righteousness or justice will stand against the truth those young eyes reveal.

And so, we must turn to the children when we seek to shape our lives with a forgiving heart. Do we comfort them? Do we warm them? Do we allow the gentle winds of faith and hope to blow through their lives? Do we teach them to love?

No measure is stronger. No measure is more pure.

By our actions we show the children how to live. By our witness, we show them what to believe.

Jesus said, "It is not the will of my Father in heaven that one of these little ones should perish." There are many ways to die — in body, in spirit, in faith, in hope. The forgiving heart weeps when the light perishes in even one child's eyes.

We are the creators; we are the healers. Their young lives are shaped by our hands. We do them no justice when we hide their eyes from the cruelty in the world, for they will find it soon enough, or it will find them, and if they have not seen it, the discovery will be a betrayal, or worse, a moment of denial or despair. But neither do we do them justice when we fail to show them the beauty of a sunset, or to teach them of the healing miracle of love.

We must show them the cruelty, then teach them how to love. We must show them the injustice, then teach them how to serve. We must open their eyes to the sunset and the murmuring tides. We must teach them how to hallow life, to value kindness, to honor the strong who lift up the weak. And then we must take their hands and lead them to a high place where they can look out over the vast richness of life and recognize that it is good.

We are our brothers' and sisters' keepers. Some of our brothers and sisters lie dying in African deserts, or crying on the graves of children who died too soon. But some are gently touching the cheeks of those they love, or washing the oil from the feathers of a wounded bird. We must take the children's hands and walk among them all, placing water on the lips of the dying, candles on the graves of those who have fallen.

If we walk humbly, stopping before the beauty as well as the sadness and sorrow, the children will begin to understand the rich profusion and unending mystery of life. They will know that it is in their hands to shape the world with kindness and with love, and that it is in their hearts that the dreams for the future must be born.

To hold. To be held. To lift the children so they can feel the warming winds of love. This is how we need to forgive. This is what we must do to be forgiven.

A child's laughter is the sound of grace. A child's trusting glance is the face of faith. When we teach a child to embrace the world, we are passing along a world of forgiveness. When we make the children laugh, we are helping God's voice burst forth into song.

Epilogue

Max & Shrimp

On the night I finished this manuscript I went out for a walk along our winding dirt road. It was dark and cloudy; I could hardly see my hand in front of my face. As I came around a corner a shadow came rushing out of the woods at me.

What was it? A deer? A wolf? It all happened too quickly. But before I could catch my breath the shadow was panting and rubbing against my leg. I reached down to feel the thick, soft coat of a massive golden retriever.

The dog wagged its tail and nuzzled me. He was large and friendly, and looking for companionship. I continued my walk, and the dog tagged along.

Our road is out in the country. All of us who live on it know each other, at least by sight. I had never seen this dog before. I knew he didn't live nearby.

I stopped at a few houses, asking if anyone had seen this dog before. None of them had.

When I returned home I brought the dog in and offered it some water. He was huge — easily a hundred pounds — and completely gray around the muzzle. His feet were splayed out in a comically slew-footed manner. He was wonderfully well behaved — someone's pet, dearly loved, and surely dearly missed.

I made a few phone calls to dog lovers I knew. None knew of an ancient golden retriever with a gray muzzle and splayed feet.

Then I tried the local police. "Oh, yes," they said. "A woman has been calling. She's very upset. This is going to make her very happy." They gave me her phone number. "By the way," they said, "The dog's name is Max."

"His name is Max," I shouted to my son, who had taken it upon himself to serve as the dog's host while he was our houseguest. I could hear the two of them talking and tussling as I made the call.

Yes, she had lost her dog. Yes, it sounded like him. Oh, she certainly hoped so. She'd be right over.

I kept the dog in the garage and sent my son to the end of our road to wait, so the woman would not drive past by mistake.

In about a quarter of an hour I saw a set of headlights moving slowly among the trees. I heard my son's muffled voice, and he came running up the driveway followed by the woman's car.

"Come on, Max," I shouted into the garage. "You've got a visitor."

Max came shambling out, saw his owner, and rushed over to her, wagging his whole backside. She threw her arms around his neck, buried her head in his coat and sobbed.

"Has he been lost long?" I asked. She tried to answer, but she was so choked with tears, I could barely understand her.

This was not a moment for conversation. She was reunited with her dog; that was enough. I retreated to a respectful distance so they could have the privacy of their own emotions.

After many hugs and tears and licks and wags, the woman stood up and looked at me with grateful eyes. She took out her purse. "Can I . . . ?"

"Of course not," I interrupted. "What more could I want than to see you and Max this happy."

She sniffled out a few "thank you's," but her heart was with her dog. Clearly, this was her best friend in life, and in her joy she could hardly be present to anyone else. She and Max climbed in the car, and drove down our driveway, and into the night.

Off to the side, almost unnoticed, my son stood, watching.

As we walked back into the house I could see he was thinking.

"She sure was happy," he said.

"It's not often you can bring someone tears of joy," I said.

He nodded, and went off to bed.

What a wonderful moment. There is no simpler happiness than watching a lost pet be reunited with its owner. How lucky my son and I were. We had witnessed a moment of joy and love, and we had played a part in creating it.

We are not always so lucky. It could have been a dead dog by the side of the road. It could have been a little spotted dog chained to a fence.

Those, too, would have been shaping moments. And those, too, would have been ours to claim.

But the cup that was passed us was sweet, and for that I will forever be grateful.

I thought about this as I placed the finished manuscript in an envelope. I had promised to send a copy to my friend John. After all, it was he who had challenged me to write about forgiveness. It was his encounter with the little spotted dog that had sparked the entire project.

Once more, I picked up my pen and began to write:

🐚

Dear John,

Here it is — the slow unraveling of my thoughts on the difficult subject of forgiveness. It has not been an easy task. Forgiveness is a delicate alloy. Too much justice, and it becomes too hard. Too much mercy, and it becomes weak and brittle. I hope I've struck the proper balance.

And now, having taken up your challenge, I want to issue one to you.

Tonight I found a dog. Not a little spotted one chained to a fence, but a big golden one wandering on the road. I got lucky: the owner was easy to find and she loved her dog deeply. Nick stood by and watched as the woman and her dog shared a joyful reunion. Somewhere there is a happy woman and a happy dog tonight, and Nick is going to sleep with a vision of kindness in his heart.

What about your daughter? What vision is she taking to bed with her these nights? Does she still see the image of a little spotted dog chained to a fence? Does she still hear her father saying, "I'll think of something," while the little spotted dog sleeps uncared for and unloved several blocks away?

Those are harsh questions, but this is a harsh world. We don't always get easy answers and happy endings. Some of us get big golden dogs with kind, appreciative owners. Some of us get little spotted dogs and motorcycle thugs who throw beer cans on their lawns.

You got the little spotted dog. What are you going to do? You can't turn away. This is yours. You may not have chosen this moment, but it has chosen you. You, alone, are the father to your child. You, alone, stand before that hopeful little dog chained to a fence. You, alone, of all the people who have ever lived, have in your hands the power to shape that moment into something good — for your daughter, for that little spotted dog, for your own heart and spirit.

How are you going to lead your daughter to embrace a world that offers little spotted dogs chained to fences as readily as it offers up tearful reunions of floppy golden retrievers and loving owners?

How are you going to make that encounter with the little spotted dog an occasion of hope and promise that your daughter will carry in her and pass on to her children, who will pass it along to their children, to the seventh generation?

This is the challenge before you. It is the wager of your life contained in a single moment. What are you going to do? And how are you going to do it?

Kent

❧

I almost didn't include the letter. But, in the end, I did. What good are words if they don't lead us to action?

A week later a response arrived. It was much smaller than I'd expected — a thank you note–sized envelope addressed in a child's hand. Inside was a single sheet of lined notebook paper folded around a photo.

❧

Dear Mr. Nerburn,

Thank you for writing that book. My dad really likes it. He read me the part about the dog you found. I really like it.

We have a new dog. It is just a puppy. It belonged to the neighbors. They were mean. My dad got me some dog treats and we went to their house. They said they didn't want the dog.

Well, I've got to go now. Bye.

P.S. We named it Shrimp. My dad wanted to name it Kent but my mom thought that was stupid.

❧

I looked at the photo. It was John and his family. He and his wife were standing behind. Their daughter was sitting in front with a big gap-toothed grin. Shrimp was sitting on her lap, looking like the happiest dog who ever lived.

I turned the photo over. On the back, in John's handwriting, was a short note.

" 'Forgiveness isn't something we give or receive. It's something we create.' Thanks, Kent."

Then, in tiny letters on the bottom,
"Want to dog-sit for a couple weeks this summer?"

About the Author

Kent Nerburn received his Ph.D. in religion and art from the Graduate Theological Union in conjunction with the University of California at Berkeley. Formerly a sculptor of religious art, with sculptures in such places as Westminster Benedictine Abbey in Mission, British Columbia, and the Peace Museum in Hiroshima, Japan, he now devotes himself to crafting books. He is the author of *Simple Truths, Small Graces, Letters to My Son, Neither Wolf nor Dog, Make Me an Instrument of Your Peace, and Road Angels.* He is also the editor of several books of Native American wisdom.

He lives with his family in Bemidji, Minnesota. His website is www.kentnerburn.com.

New World Library publishes books and other forms of
communication that inspire and challenge us to
improve our lives and our world.

Our books and audio and video cassettes
are in bookstores everywhere.
For a catalog of our complete library
of publications, contact:

New World Library
14 Pamaron Way
Novato, CA 94949

Telephone: (415) 884-2100
Fax: (415) 884-2199
Toll free: (800) 972-6657
Catalog requests: Ext. 50
Ordering: Ext. 52

E-mail: escort@nwlib.com
www.newworldlibrary.com